The Essential Guide to Business Communication for Finance Professionals

The Essential Guide to Business Communication for Finance Professionals

Jason L. Snyder and Lisa A.C. Frank

BEP BUSINESS EXPERT PRESS

The Essential Guide to Business Communication for Finance Professionals

First published in 2016 by
Business Expert Press, LLC
222 East 46th Street, New York, NY 10017
www.businessexpertpress.com

ISBN-13: 978-1-63157-353-8 (paperback)
ISBN-13: 978-1-63157-354-5 (e-book)

Business Expert Press Corporate Communication Collection

Collection ISSN: 2156-8162 (print)
Collection ISSN: 2156-8170 (electronic)

Cover and interior design by Exeter Premedia Services Private Ltd., Chennai, India

First edition: 2016

10 9 8 7 6 5 4 3 2 1

Printed in the United States of America.

Abstract

Communication skills are a competitive advantage for today's finance professionals. It is truly the cave dweller who still believes that math skills are the only requirement for success in the finance industry. Savvy professionals know that employers want and need employees with excellent relationship building, writing, and presentation skills. They also understand that the market demand for exceptional communication skills is going unmet. *The Essential Guide to Business Communication for Finance Professionals* asks its readers to adopt the "communicate or die" philosophy in their approach to their careers. Two business professors with years of experience in finance and communication offer advice and tips for approaching some of the most common business communication situations faced by today's finance professionals. Readers will walk away from this book with tools that can be applied immediately to manage their professional image and reputation. The advice and tips are enhanced through the use of real-world examples and quotes from professionals working in the finance field.

Keywords

business communication, business messages, business presentations, business writing, career advice, communication, finance, managerial communication, relationship building

Contents

Foreword

Are you ready to launch your career by taking advantage of a skills gap in the finance field? Employers believe that relationship building, writing, and speaking skills are sorely lacking among today's young finance professionals. In this book, we endeavor to give you the tools you need to build your professional reputation and demonstrate your communication skills. We ask you to adopt the "communicate or die" philosophy to business communication and take personal responsibility for your professional image and career trajectory. In a few short hours, you will learn how to (a) enhance your professional relationships, (b) apply the secrets of effective business communicators, (c) overcome the barriers to effective business communication, (d) become a more disciplined writer, and (e) demonstrate the traits of a virtuous presenter. If you start reading the book now, you will be able to put what you learn to use before the end of the day.

Acknowledgments

We owe a debt of gratitude to all those people who helped us turn our vision for this book into a reality. In particular, we would like to thank those individuals who responded to our interview questions about their communication experiences in the finance profession. Their input added context and credibility to this book. Their responses and experiences are what make this book one that is truly directed at finance professionals rather than yet another broad-brush approach to professional communication. Our sincere thanks go to Vincent Finelli, Constance Myles, Rob Casella, Eric Bergenn, Peter Bianco, Matthew House, and Jennifer Savini. In addition, we owe a special thank you to Michael Hammerslag who offered his assistance in a number of ways and who acted as a consultant on this project.

CHAPTER 1

Embracing the "Communicate or Die" Philosophy in Finance

The good news is that we certainly don't think you'll literally die if you don't embrace the communication lessons we share with you in this book. To torture a phrase from Shakespeare's *Hamlet*, however, you may shuffle off your professional coil if you close this book now without taking heed of the advice we are about to share. We hope that for the sake of your career you will forge ahead!

This book is intended for finance professionals in the early stages of their careers. Even if you're not in that demographic, we promise that you will learn a few new tricks. If you are in our target audience, then the publisher has done a good job of marketing this book. We hope you're asking yourself why you should be reading this book. After all, you're a professional in a data-driven, number-crunching profession who has also most likely taken English composition and public speaking in college. Why read a book on professional communication? What's the point? We look forward to answering those questions in this chapter.

Jason, who holds a PhD in Communication Science, has taught communication courses for nearly 15 years on topics such as organizational communication, managerial communication, and (ahem) public speaking. Lisa brings a dozen years of professional finance experience and a PhD in Finance to the classroom, where she has, for nearly 15 years, been teaching finance to undergraduate and graduate students. Between the two of us, we have heard your questions hundreds—if not thousands—of times. So, let's spend some time here in Chapter 1 addressing those questions. By the end of the chapter, we hope you'll come to understand that professional communication skills:

- Include more than basic composition and public speaking
- Are in low supply and high demand in the finance industry
- Will give you a competitive advantage throughout your career

English Composition and Public Speaking Are Not Enough

As we said before, you've probably taken one or two English composition classes while you were in college. In fact, before you started your career, you probably wrote a number of papers for your college classes. If you haven't started your professional career, then we have a secret to share with you. College writing is *not* the same thing as writing for a professional audience. Many of the lessons you learned about writing simply don't apply. Those of you with more work experience may have already figured that out. That said, we do not advise you fire off an angry missive to your former professors for wasting your time. They taught you a number of valuable lessons about writing. We argue that the factors highlighted in Table 1.1 constitute major differences between the writing you did in college and the writing you should do in your career. The best business communicators understand these factors.

The writing you produced in college was written for a professor. Not all professors are the same. So, one valuable lesson you learned from those writing experiences is that you have to always put your audience first. You know that you need to make your audience happy. That's a lesson you should carry with you throughout your career and a point we come back to repeatedly throughout this book.

Table 1.1 Major differences between compositional and professional writing

	Compositional	Professional
Primary audience	Professor	Varies, depending on situation
Voice	Passive	Active
Tone	Formal	Conversational
Length	Longer	Shorter
Purpose	Demonstrate knowledge and thinking	Inform and persuade

In business writing, however, you usually communicate to busy professionals whose jobs don't typically include evaluating your writing skills (although that doesn't mean they don't judge you). These professionals need you to get to the point so they can move on with their days. In many cases, you are not writing for a single audience. You are also writing for secondary audiences. The people who write annual reports are not writing for an individual, but for a number of audiences, including investors and regulators. Financial planners help clients with their financial affairs. Their audience often includes people with very limited knowledge of finance. In large organizations, internal memos and reports must be written for multiple audiences within the organization who have varying degrees of expertise in finance. Although you must always make your audience happy, that task can be substantially more difficult in business because your audience is often fragmented and diverse.

Don't just take our word for it. Vincent Finelli is a 26-year-old finance professional who holds an MBA and has two years' experience as a risk analyst for a global commodities trading firm. He talked with us about the importance of understanding his audience. In his work, he communicates with colleagues from around the globe. As a result, it is critical for him to avoid jargon, slang, and idioms in his communications because he needs to be sensitive to language and cultural differences. Additionally, his job places highly private financial information at his disposal. As a result, he has to be aware of his audience because oversharing this information in the trading environment is accompanied by business and legal

Vincent Finelli
Risk Analyst
Global Commodities Trading Firm

implications. There are few one-size-fits-all communication scenarios he faces because his audience is always so diverse. His heightened awareness of these communication issues has allowed him to tailor his communications. Communicating in a diverse environment where language and cultural differences exist were not part of his undergraduate writing experience.[1]

Because your audience is different in business than that in college, the tone of your messages will be affected. Compositional writing taught in college usually stresses passive voice and formal tone. Business writing prefers active voice and conversational tone. We describe passive voice in greater detail later in the book. For now, suffice it to say that passive voice follows an object–verb–subject pattern. Active voice follows the subject–verb–object pattern. In other words, active voice sentences tell us who did what to whom (or what). Active voice sentences are generally clearer and easier to understand.

Consider the following simple example: *Lisa ran a half marathon.* As some of you may know, running a half marathon is not easy. In this case, our author Lisa has actually run a half marathon. That's a major accomplishment for which she deserves credit. The active sentence places emphasis on the subject (Lisa), gives her credit, and makes it easy for the reader to know who did what to whom (or what). If we write the same sentence in passive voice, it would read one of two ways:

- *A half marathon was run by Lisa.*
- *A half marathon was run.*

Both passive sentences place the emphasis on the object (half marathon). The second passive sentence excludes the subject (Lisa). Given how hard she worked to train for and run a half marathon, Lisa would not be happy losing the credit for her accomplishment.

Your college professors wanted you to demonstrate the quality and depth of your thinking when writing essays and reports. That usually resulted in long papers. Remember how they always asked you for—sigh—page minimums? That approach served its purpose. However, your professional audiences don't have that kind of time. They want you to provide the necessary information, make your request, or provide your recommendation. As long as you can demonstrate that you've done your research, this audience prefers that you get to the point sooner, rather than later. In fact, Jason's assignments to his managerial communication students have page maximums, because if you can't make your point succinctly, then your audience won't care to finish reading your tome. Save the thesis for the classroom.

Composition classes are not sufficient for making you an effective business writer, and public speaking classes are not sufficient for making you an effective business presenter. Why isn't a public speaking class sufficient for developing the presentation skills you need for your career? In public speaking, you learned—we hope—about organizing your thoughts, supporting points with evidence, and the importance of an extemporaneous style (i.e., not reading your presentation from notes). Those are all valuable lessons. However, for most of us, the vast majority of our professional presentations will be delivered to small audiences, often fewer than 10 people. Public speaking courses do not prepare you for delivering a presentation to a small audience in a boardroom. They do not prepare you for the unique challenges of the business context, including presenting financial statements to managers, making budget recommendations, participating in quarterly report calls to investors, selling a new product, pitching a product to investors, defending an unpopular decision to employees, or teaching nonfinancial managers how to explain financial data to lay audiences.

The point here is that you need to approach writing and speaking in a different way than you have in the past. This book will help you develop the skills you need to be an effective business communicator. The next thing we have to do, however, is to explain to you why you should care about being an effective business communicator.

Business Communication Skills and Your Career

People believe they are effective communicators. It makes sense. We all communicate all day long for our entire lives. We all have years of experience. Unfortunately, having lots of experience does not always make you better. If you do something wrong a million times, you're still doing it wrong.

Most of your peers believe they are already effective communicators and will never seek the guidance necessary to go from bad to good or good to great. As a result, those people are presenting you with a competitive advantage. Let's take a closer look at the advantage they're providing you and on which you are now capitalizing. You're finance people, so we should probably show you some numbers now.

How many of your peers believe they are effective communicators? The Hart Research Associates, on behalf of the Association of American Colleges and Universities, recently conducted a nationwide study of more than 400 large employers and more than 600 recent college graduates about career readiness. When those graduates were asked if they were well prepared for work in terms of their communication skills, do you know what they said? Not surprisingly, they reported feeling prepared. In fact, 62% felt their oral communication skills were adequate and 65% felt the same way about their writing skills.

Although we're college professors and would love to take this opportunity to pat ourselves on the back, that would be premature. In the same study, employers were asked about the preparedness of recent college graduates. Their outlook on the situation was less rosy. A mere 28% of employers reported that recent college graduates have adequate oral communication skills, and 27% felt that way about written communication skills.[2]

Do you see the disconnect? Young professionals tend to believe they are good communicators. Their employers disagree. How do you feel about your written and oral communication skills? How do you think your employer feels? How much do written and oral communication skills matter, anyway? We're glad you asked. Here's a hint, we wrote a book about the importance of communication skills for young finance professionals.

Employers do, in fact, care about your communication skills. According to its 2015 survey of employers, the National Association of Colleges and Employers (NACE) found that 85% of employers said oral communication skills were sought in recent graduates, although 73% of employers indicated that written communication skills were important.[3] Moreover, the NACE college graduate career readiness task force, comprising representatives from major employers and universities, cited oral

and written communication skills as one of seven competencies that prepare students for a successful transition from school to work.[4] Employers
in the Hart Research Associates study nearly universally agreed that skills
including communication, critical thinking, and problem solving are
more important to career success than is a student's major.[5]

A 2015 *USA Today* article reported on a CareerBuilder survey of
employers. Their findings should lend even more kindling to the fire we
hope is beginning to build inside you about capitalizing on the competitive advantage gained through focus on communication skills. Of the
top five soft skills cited in the CareerBuilder study, oral communication
skills ranked #3 and written communication skills ranked #5. The article's
author reports that

> while many companies have open positions and are eager to hire,
> they report having trouble finding qualified candidates to fill those
> positions. Twenty-one percent of employers surveyed by Career-
> Builder said they didn't feel that colleges were doing enough to
> prepare students for the working world. ... employers are trou-
> bled by graduates' lack of soft skills.[6]

And this advice applies to professionals from all fields, including finance.
In fact, a recent article on finance job skills made the case for the importance of communication skills in the finance industry. The authors argued:

> Finance jobs require skills in communicating policies and pro-
> cedures to other employees and customers. Finance profession-
> als should be able to present the budget to staff members and
> explain why there is a profit or loss. Finance positions in a bank
> or investment firm include communicating with customers on a
> regular basis and answering questions about financial transactions.
> During meetings and conferences, executive finance professionals
> make presentations on the financial health of a company to other
> staff, board members and potential clients.[7]

Written and oral communication skills are important for helping you
be effective in your work, but the benefits of effective communication

don't end there. Your communication skills influence the impressions that you make on others. In fact, this is a skill we call impression management. Whether you like it or not, other people form opinions about your professional character based on whatever information they have about you. Your communication skills can help you manage or mismanage the impression that others form. A 2014 York College study on professionalism asked university career development professionals what qualities best represent a recent graduate's professionalism. Fifty-six percent of the respondents made a reference to communication skills.[8]

Do you remember when we asked you about your employer's impression of your communication skills? The odds suggest that your employer doesn't think much of your written and oral communication skills. But how does your employer see you as a professional?

The York College of Pennsylvania 2014 National Professionalism Survey of Career Development Professionals points to technology as a major reason for a decrease in professionalism due to its negative effect on focus and interpersonal and communication skills.[9] Millennials generally expect that they can freely communicate with friends via text and social media during working hours.[10] Furthermore, the perception is that the majority of millennials abuse technology and circumvent company IT policies.[11] It should come as no surprise that millennials are cited as the generation most lacking in qualities of professionalism.[12] Regardless of whether the perceptions of millennials are accurate, the perceptions exist and are pervasive in the modern workplace. We interviewed a finance professional with 17 years' experience who presently works as a vice president for a broadband communications firm. He said:

> There is a clear distinction in workplace communication with Millennials compared to their more experienced colleagues. This is particularly evident in the use of smart phones and instant messaging. Millennials can often be noticed working on their computer while multi-tasking on their smart phones via headsets (i.e. listening to music) or text messaging. While the preferred medium for conversation and exchange of information with more experienced colleagues is face-to-face discussions, phone conversations and e-mails, such experienced colleagues are finding it more efficient and impactful to communicate with their millennial counterparts

in quick, fact based, concise messages via smart phone/texting. In an almost perceived avoidance of face-to-face conversations, web based meetings and screen sharing are also becoming prevalent with younger colleagues as well.[13]

And although we professors may be loath to admit it, perhaps colleges and universities aren't doing enough to help students develop these key soft skills. Many business schools don't require communication courses beyond those included in general education requirements. The common business core tends to be heavy in quantitative skills.

In addition to courses, however, universities do offer career services and development opportunities. But many students aren't taking advantage of those opportunities. The 2014 York College study on workplace professionalism concluded that few students use career development programs, with only 53% of students using those services in their senior year (and far fewer using those services prior to senior year).[14] In fact, our university offers skill development workshops, such as the one advertised in Figure 1.1.

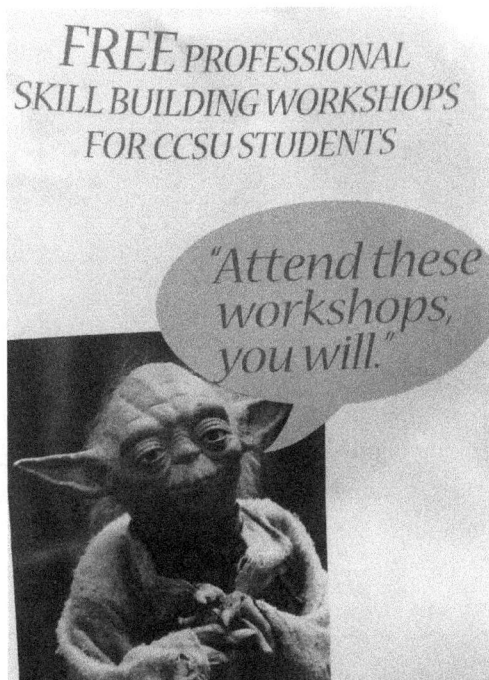

Figure 1.1 Skills workshop flyer

Attendance at these events is usually paltry, however. If college coursework doesn't prepare students and only half of all students bother to use career development programs, it's no wonder students enter the workplace without the necessary skills to succeed.

Conclusion

By now, we hope that we've answered your questions about why you should read this book and put its lessons into practice (see Box 1.1). Communication skills are highly desired in business, particularly in the finance industry; the communication skills you picked up through college coursework are not sufficient; most of your peers believe they have the necessary communication skills to succeed but their employers disagree; your communication skills influence the impressions others form about you; and few people take advantage of the professional development opportunities presented to them. For all of these reasons, we argue that developing your communication skills will give you a competitive advantage in your career. So many careers are needlessly on life support. Embracing the "communicate or die" philosophy will help ensure a long, healthy career.

Box 1.1 *Chapter 1 takeaways*

1. Finance employers want employees with better communication skills.
2. The communication skills you developed in college are not sufficient.
3. Most people believe they possess the communication skills needed to succeed.
4. Employers do not believe their inexperienced employees have adequate communication skills.
5. Most of your peers do not take advantage of professional development opportunities related to communication.
6. Embracing the "communicate or die" philosophy will give you a competitive advantage.

CHAPTER 2

Using the Secrets of Effective Business Communication

As you'll recall from Chapter 1, we tried to justify our existence and also describe the competitive advantage afforded to those who work to improve their business communication skills. What separates the best communicators from the rest of us? This question was posed by Anne Grinols, a nationally recognized professor of business communication, at a discussion during the 2010 convention of the Association for Business Communication.[1] Those in attendance, including Jason, discussed what they'd observed and what they'd learned from research. As a result, Jason crafted a lecture that he calls the secrets of effective business communication. He's delivered the lecture for his students as well as during a number of invited presentations. In this chapter, we share with you the ten secrets and how they can be applied to your professional life.

Before diving into the secrets, however, we should tell you what we mean when we talk about effective business communication. Effective business communication must accomplish two goals: (1) Your audience must understand your message, and (2) your audience must respond the way you want them to respond. Both of these goals matter and they should be accomplished while fulfilling the ABCs of effective business communication: accuracy, brevity, and clarity (we address the ABCs later in the book). For instance, it's not enough for your employer to understand you when you ask for a raise and then not give it to you. In addition to meeting these two goals, effective business communicators practice the following ten secrets.

Secret 1: Communication = Relationships

We thought an equation might get your attention. One of the first secrets of effective business communicators is that they understand the principle that communication is about relationships. In order to help you arrive at that conclusion, we need to first discuss what we mean by communication. Although what we're about to discuss will sound like definitions, it's important to remember that there are no right or wrong definitions. One of Jason's professors used to say that some definitions are more useful than others. Definitions provide limits and frame our ways of thinking about a subject.

Many books begin their discussion of communication by providing readers with a picture of the basic process. In that process, person A sends a message to person B, who then responds in some way. Those models, which we discuss later in the book, are a great way to learn about how communication works and what kinds of barriers communicators confront. They help us think about the nuts and bolts of communication. For now, however, we want you to think beyond the communication model.

There are literally hundreds of definitions for communication. Rather than get into the weeds, we direct you to a few resources.[2,3] We point out, however, some important distinctions about how communication is defined.

The first distinction is between definitions that describe communication as purely symbolic and definitions that include spontaneous and pseudo-spontaneous signs. Symbolic communication is intentional and is usually associated with written and oral communication. The words and numbers we use are symbols that we put to intentional use. The e-mail that a financial planner sends to a client contains symbols and is intended to send a specific message. Communicators intentionally construct messages to be conveyed to their audiences. Definitions focused on symbolic interaction describe communication as discrete.[4]

Other definitions of communication move beyond symbolic interaction to include spontaneous and pseudo-spontaneous messages.[5] Spontaneous messages include emotional responses to stimuli. For example, the stunned look on a stockholder's face when he learns of a sudden and precipitous drop in stock price. Pseudo-spontaneous communication includes false and intentional representations of emotion. An employee is taking part in pseudo-spontaneous communication when the boss fires her but she doesn't show any visible emotional reaction. She is intentionally displaying (or not displaying) an emotional reaction to send a specific message. In this case, she's trying to send the message that she's unaffected.

We prefer the definitions that include symbolic, spontaneous, and pseudo-spontaneous messages. Symbolic communication is important, especially in the United States where business is conducted in a low-context culture that wants everything in writing. The symbolic message is really important. However, we believe that spontaneous and pseudo-spontaneous messages influence the nature of what is being communicated symbolically. For example, consider that employee we mentioned in the preceding text who has been fired. Does the nature of that message change if the person doing the firing has a giant grin on his face while delivering this sobering news? The spontaneous and pseudo-spontaneous messages matter. And they affect the nature of the relationship. Effective business communicators are aware of all three messages and how they impact their business relationships.

The other important distinction between communication definitions is whether communication is viewed as an event or a process. We follow the definition that communication is processual in nature.[6] Our messages don't take place in a vacuum. The last e-mail you sent at work or school was an event in a much larger process. You were responding to something.

Communication is patterned over space and time.[7] As an example, we all follow basic social scripts. We all say good morning to our coworkers and customers. The situation may vary (e.g., the words we use, the gestures we use), but the basic pattern stays the same. We were recently at a presentation where the speaker played a YouTube video of the many different versions of the song "Besame Mucho." The notes followed the same pattern between versions, but the arrangement changed. Similarly, communication follows patterns but can still be different from one situation to the next.

Thinking about communication as an ongoing process also acknowledges the role communication plays in building and maintaining healthy relationships. The process approach recognizes the interdependent nature of communication. This approach allows us to avoid dehumanizing our audiences, acknowledge the important role of relationships in our professional lives, and understand the interdependence and mutual influence that truly characterize our dealings with others.[8]

Imagine that you are trying to sell a product to your customer and that customer frowns, leans back in her chair, and crosses her arms. Do you think, "This is going great; I won't change a thing"? Probably not. You're more likely to think that things aren't going so well and it's time to change the pitch. But what if you've worked with this customer for years and happen to know that this customer is quiet, thoughtful, and rarely smiles? Your history with that person may, in fact, lead you to an entirely different interpretation of the communication episode.

Another common example is the business colleague who always tries to dominate discussion during meetings. Each time this person acts in a domineering way, you can either submit to that style or push back. Your choice will be affected by your past experiences in meetings and with this colleague. In turn, these factors and your choice to use a one up (push back) or one down (submit) tactic in response to domineering behavior will influence how your colleague responds. In both of these examples, the relationship has influenced the communication process and vice versa.

Try This at Home

Another fun way to test the interdependent nature of communication is to take a friend to dinner. During the course of your conversation, hold a particular posture, such as elbows on table and fingers interlocked in front of your face. By the end of dinner, your friend will likely mimic that behavior.

So, communication is a process including symbolic, spontaneous, and pseudo-spontaneous messages in which the parties involved are interdependent and able to influence one another. What does that imply? Why does it matter?

The great communicators have come to understand that communication is really about the building and maintaining of relationships. In other words, communication is the sine qua non of relationships. Expressed another way, relationships do not exist without communication. Edna Rogers put it best, "The concept of a relationship implies some form of interconnection between different sets of events, individuals, or entities; in essence it refers to an interconnectedness of differences."[9] Your reputation, your history with others, the things you have done in the past, and many other factors impact your relationships with others. Relationships exist only if we first communicate.

Think about your own industry. Do you think relationships are important? How do you build and maintain relationships that will help you succeed in your career? The first step is understanding that communication matters. You can't have relationships without communication, and the quality of your communication translates to the quality of your relationships. Vincent Finelli, the risk analyst you met in Chapter 1, put it nicely, "Professional relationships are everything in a corporate environment. You need to be a hard worker, but most importantly you need to fit in with your colleagues."

So, it's important to understand that in a world where relationships matter, your communication skills will largely determine the quality of those relationships. We understand that you won't always have good news to share with those you encounter in your professional lives, and some people will test the limits of your grace and good nature. We are not suggesting that you have to be a 24-hour-a-day ray of sunshine, but that you need to be aware of how your communication behaviors affect your professional relationships. You can deliver bad news without being bad. The person you say no to today may be the person from whom you need help tomorrow.

Secret 2: People Are Busy

Effective business communicators understand that other people are busy, and it's important to respect others' time. We all are bombarded by messages and information that are demanding of our attention. E-mails, voice mails, phone calls, instant messages, reports, memos, meetings, and other communications beckon our attention. We simply can't keep up. As a result, we ignore some things and pay attention to others.

According to a recent study, new MBA hires send and receive approximately 200 e-mail messages each day.[10] A 2014 *Harvard Business Review* article stated the typical executive receives 30,000 e-mails per year.[11] The average worker in the United States spends 650 hours writing more than 41,000 words in e-mails each year.[12] In addition, the average worker attends 62 meetings per month.[13] A 2016 study of one large organization concluded that one weekly meeting of midlevel managers resulted in a $15 million per year cost to the organization.[14] And sometimes we check e-mail while attending meetings, which is also a waste of time because multitasking decreases our productivity.[15] So much of our work time is not seen as a resource, and much of it is wasted as a result. The authors of a recent article in the *Harvard Business Review* expressed the problem this way:

> Most companies have no clear understanding of how their leaders and employees are spending their collective time. Not surprisingly, that time is often squandered—on long e-mail chains, needless conference calls, and countless unproductive meetings. This takes a heavy toll. Time devoted to internal meetings detracts from time spent with customers. Organizations become bloated, bureaucratic, and slow, and their financial performance suffers. Employees spend an ever-increasing number of hours away from their families and friends, with little to show for it.[16]

We recently interviewed Ms. Connie Myles who has 26 years of experience in finance and currently works as a Director of Financial Planning and Analysis for a major telecommunications firm. She told us that in her experience:

> Respecting people's time is a message that really resonates with me. I never take my cell phone into a meeting. Yet, in almost every meeting I attend, as I look around the room, there are many individuals skimming their emails during a colleague's presentation. It sends the message that their time is more important than that of the presenter.[17]

Every piece of communication impinges on our senses, like any other stimulus that impinges on our senses. If we tried to keep up with every piece of information communicated to us, we would go insane! To highlight this point, think about all of your senses. At any given moment, all of those senses are being impinged upon. Do you pay attention to every little stimulus? Of course not, your body would freak out.

For example, think about the socks on your feet. They impinge upon your senses every second of the day. Does that mean you are constantly and consciously aware of how they feel at all times? No. You do not pay attention to that information. It is usually unimportant and not salient. Except for right now. We bet you can feel those socks at this very moment. Our point is that just as your body can't consciously think about those socks all of the time, your mind can't process all of the information that is being communicated to you. As a result, we all use selective perception processes to help us pay attention to important information and filter out everything else.

Connie Myles
Director of Financial Planning
and Analysis
Telecommunications Firm

Great business communicators know they have to make a choice to either (a) find a way to make messages stand out or (b) risk having communications ignored, like the socks of the communication world. Great communicators understand that people are busy, place a value on time, and find ways to respect time and get attention. Ms. Myles put it best when she told us:

> People with good communication skills will excel in comparison to those with poor communication skills. If one tends to fly below the radar, no matter how smart he may be, he will never be recognized for his efforts. One needs to be able to present their findings whether written or verbally. Great leaders are great communicators. They connect with their teams. They keep their teams engaged.[18]

Communicating concisely is important to respecting people's time. It's important to be clear and brief. Every word we use takes time. Every time we make an error in communication, we lose time in correcting that error and we waste our audience's time by creating confusion. Although there are a number of ways that we can respect others' time and get attention, we offer some advice you can follow in two areas: meetings and e-mails.

Effective meetings are all about the planning. We like to listen to the advice of efficiency and productivity guru Merlin Mann when it comes to meetings. From his speeches, we can take away a few simple lessons.[19]

- *Hold meetings only when necessary.* We shouldn't hold a meeting simply because our team traditionally meets on the first Wednesday of the month. Have a purpose.
- *Invite to meetings only those who need attend.* Again, we tend to invite people out of tradition. Think about the agenda and who *really* needs to be in attendance. Consider how you would respond to each person on the guest list if he or she asked, "Why should I be there?"
- *Let people know what they should do to be prepared for the meeting.*
- *Show up prepared.* Think about how annoying it is to sit in a meeting and wait while an unprepared colleague shuffles through notes or can't find information that would have been readily available with a little preparation.

- *Stay on task and stay on time.* If you schedule a meeting to conclude at 10 a.m., then finish at 10 a.m. Be thorough in how you plan out the time.

Beyond face-to-face communication, research and (too much) experience tells us that e-mail is the preferred channel of communication in the modern work environment. As noted already, this leads to abusive e-mail behavior. Here are some rules to improve your use of e-mail that respects others' time and gets your communications noticed.

- *Write short, actionable subject lines.* Consider using two words at the beginning of the subject line that tell the reader some action is required. For example, "Please Advise." Such subject lines let the reader know he or she must do something other than simply read the message. You know you delete e-mails without opening them. If you don't believe you have a reason to open an e-mail, you won't. It may be a dirty little communication secret, but there's no reason to pretend that other people won't delete your messages if they aren't compelled to read them.
- *Use the top-of-screen test.* Newspapers put their best headlines above the fold on the first page, because that gets people's attention. We should practice the same principle in our e-mails. Try to put your request and the most vital pieces of information at the top of your message, preferably in an area that covers less than half the computer—or mobile device—screen (see Figure 2.1). Due to common e-mail interfaces that default to providing e-mail content on only half the screen, readers often skim messages and move on without looking past that first half screen unless they feel compelled to do so. If you don't make your point in the first few lines, it will likely be overlooked.
- *Use bulleted and numbered lists.* Another way to make important pieces of information stand out in an e-mail is to offset it in a bulleted or numbered list. Use lists only for important pieces of information. Remember the following

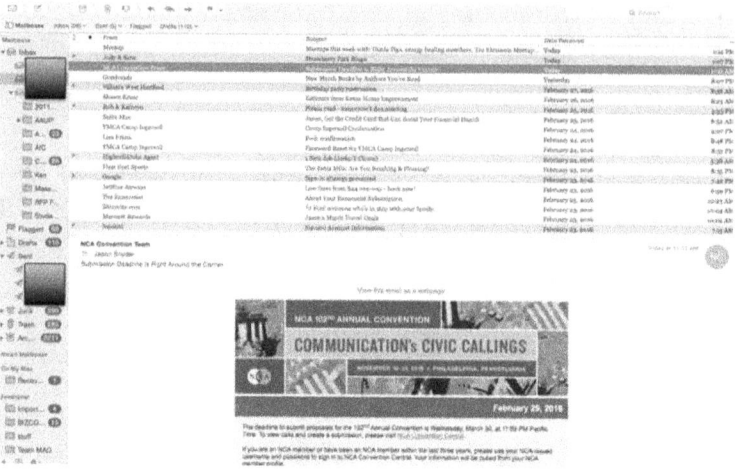

Figure 2.1 Busy inbox requiring you to pass top-of-screen test

rule about lists: *If everything is important, then nothing is important.*

- **Pick unique times to send messages, when possible.** Think about a time when you might send the message and have it appear at the top of the receiver's inbox—like sending it at 8:30 a.m. if the person arrives at work at 9 a.m. A colleague of Jason's recently commented that he was surprised to see that Jason sends him e-mails at 4 a.m. Jason may not sleep much, but his colleague reads those messages.

- **Don't hide behind your e-mail.** Sometimes an e-mail simply isn't an effective means for communicating your message. Great communicators understand that point. Relationships often require you to get out from behind the monitor and interact with the people around you. Remember Secret #1? At times, e-mail can damage a professional relationship. E-mail is inappropriate when you need to consider others' feelings, when you are angry, or when you need to make sure you are understood.[20]

- **Avoid overusing "cc" and "bcc."** Just as with meetings, please send information only to people who need that information. Wasting others' time by copying them unnecessarily is a sin to the effective business communicator.

Secret 3: Each Communication Carries Two Messages

When we communicate with others, we are implicitly negotiating the nature of our relationship (Secret #1) with others. It's a truism of communication and completely unavoidable. In their famous (in communication nerd circles, anyway) 1967 book, Paul Watzlawick, Janet Beavin, and Don Jackson discussed five rules of communication that are always true (see Box 2.1). As you can see, we have already discussed Rules 4 and 5. In this section, we address Rules 1 and 2.

Let's first discuss this idea that "one cannot not communicate." Ignore the grammar in that sentence and focus on what that sentence means. Any behavior that can be perceived by someone else has the potential to communicate. Therefore, we can't avoid communicating with others when we find ourselves in the same social space. We are continually communicating information about ourselves, our reaction to others, our reaction to the situation, and our intentional messages.

For example, think about that coworker who walks past you in the hallway, puts his hands in his pockets, looks at the floor, and doesn't say a word. That person may be trying to avoid communicating with you, but that doesn't mean he hasn't communicated with you. In fact, because you perceived this behavior, you have drawn conclusions about what your coworker is "saying" to you. Depending on the context and your history with that coworker, you may draw any one of several different conclusions. Despite your coworker's efforts to avoid it, communication still occurred. So, why does this matter?

Box 2.1 Watzlawick, Beavin, and Jackson's (1967) communication rules

1. One cannot not communicate.
2. Your communications carry both content and relational messages.
3. Verbal communication has punctuation similar to nonverbal communication.
4. You communicate verbally and nonverbally.
5. The nature of the relationship you have with others influences your communication behavior.

This rule matters because the message you received was probably not the message that was intended. In fact, the message you received was likely more than what your coworker intended. People assign meaning to stimuli. They use whatever information they have available to draw conclusions about you, the situation, the relationship, and the intentional message.[21] Great business communicators understand that they are always communicating. Everything we do that can be perceived by others sends all sorts of information that can be interpreted in many ways. It's important to understand that something as simple as how you dress communicates something about you. And that leads us to Rule #2—your communications carry both content and relational messages.

In business, we tend to believe that we make rational decisions and act rationally. We underestimate the importance of emotion. We focus on the written word. Our organizations comprise people who have emotions, and those emotions matter. The words we use make up the content message we send with every communication. However, every communication carries a relational message, a message about the nature of the relationship and the relative status of those involved. These relational messages matter as much as—and sometimes more than—the content messages. Great business communicators pay careful attention to both the words they use and the context in which they're used.

For example, a colleague who is a member of a financial advisory board for a small business attends board meetings on a regular basis at which dinner and beverages are usually served. Board advisors offer their expertise to the small business during the meeting, and this has historically been viewed as a benefit to the business. However, the most recent meeting was held earlier than usual and food was not served. Clearly there is a nonverbal message here, whether intentional or not, indicating that the business no longer values the expertise of the members enough to indulge them with dinner and drinks.

Secret 4: Nonverbal Communication Needs to Complement Verbal Communication

What we say and how we say it need to complement one another. Secret #4 is closely related to Secret #3. Effective business communicators understand that when verbal and nonverbal communication do not complement or reinforce one another, greater weight is usually given to the nonverbal communication. In other words, if you say during a conversation that you're passionate about your job, but you say it in a whisper while staring at your shoes, your verbal and nonverbal behavior are not saying the same thing. The person you're talking to will be more likely to believe the nonverbal message.

Effective business communicators understand this principle and pay attention to it for a handful of reasons. First, when what we say and how we say it don't align, our messages lose clarity and can create confusion. Second, when what we say and how we say it don't line up, we lose control over our communications. The audience draws its own, often inappropriate, conclusions about the intended message.

The vice president we introduced you to in Chapter 1 shared the following insights from his own experience.

> When a verbal/non-verbal communication is aligned (i.e. "You did a great job" accompanied by a smile), the verbal cue is dominant and supported by the nonverbal cue. However, it's been my experience that when verbal and nonverbal communication are misaligned, (i.e. "You did a great job" accompanied by rolling one's eyes), the nonverbal cue becomes dominant and the verbal cue is almost dismissive. Key to anyone's career is genuine verbal face-to-face communication that delivers both key facts/information and portrays sincerity to the message receiver. This is critical to building relationships, trust and loyalty among colleagues. Once such verbal based relationship is established, written and other forms of communication are more important and actionable to the message receiver.[22]

Those insights are accurate and supported by research. Research in deception detection tells us that when we believe a coworker is being dishonest, we pay closer attention to the coworker's nonverbal behaviors. As we learned from Secret #1, our interpretation is colored by our past experiences with the coworker (among other things). Although that seems reasonable, the research tells us that we pay attention to the wrong nonverbal behaviors.[23] As a result, we are not good at detecting lies.

To be fair, benign fabrications can be used to help others save face (e.g., when your supervisor asks if you like his tie). But, by and large, we want our nonverbal communication to complement or reinforce our verbal messages.

Secret 5: You Are Not Your Audience

Are you passionate about your career in finance? Do you love numbers? Too often, you may be alone. You should not assume that the things you care about are the things your audience cares about. Our audience members' perspective just doesn't line up with our own. Even when our audience members are similar to us, they don't always necessarily see issues and problems from the same perspective. To demonstrate this concept, try playing the following game.

Try This at Home

Identify a common object, such as a pick-up truck. Ask a group of people to write down the first five things they think of when they think about pick-up trucks. Once they are done, compare lists. You're likely to see that no two lists are the same.

In finance, you talk about things like present values, future values, return on investment, and cash flows. These are fairly common concepts to you and when you talk with other finance professionals, they know what you're talking about. However, you will often have to share this "simple" information with people who do not have a background in finance. They do not share your perspective on these topics. Therefore, you will have to understand their perspective and talk about these matters from their perspective.

If you're going to be an effective communicator, you will have to learn the lesson that your perspective does not matter as much as your audience's perspective. Effective business communicators think from their audience's perspective and then write and speak about their own ideas from that perspective. What if you don't have a great deal of information about your audience? In that case, you have to approach the communication situation the way many great leaders do. A 2016 *Forbes* article argued that great leaders, such as Steve Jobs, communicate using the language of third graders. In other words, they simplify their language to the point that a third grader could comprehend most, if not all, of the content.[24]

One thing we know about all audiences is that they care about themselves more than anything else. When crafting messages, always try to answer the WIIFM question—What's In It For Me? Audiences will invariably, and often subconsciously, ask themselves the WIIFM question. So, always try to answer it. Remember how we started the book in Chapter 1 by trying to address common questions we hear about the importance of business communication? That was our first attempt to answer your WIIFM question.

Great business communicators understand that the more they know about their audience members' backgrounds, beliefs, and attitudes, the more successful they will be in engaging that audience. Learn to put your own perspective in the background and your audience's perspective in the foreground. Not only will it keep your audience engaged, it will also enhance their perception of your goodwill.

Secret 6: Communication Breakdown Does Not Exist

What does the bearded fellow in Figure 2.2 have in common with communication breakdown? Don't tell our kids, but neither really exists, and it would really upset them to know that communication breakdown isn't real. You probably hear the term communication breakdown all the time, but we implore you to purge it from your vocabulary. After all, as we learned earlier in this chapter, communication is a process. It's a made-up word with hundreds of definitions. It is not tangible.

It's our opinion that the phrase communication breakdown is commonly used to deflect blame when things go wrong. Even effective business communicators make mistakes. They encounter barriers to communication that they fail to overcome. It happens all the time. The major difference between effective business communicators and the rest of us is that they accept personal responsibility for their failures and learn from

Figure 2.2 A child posing with a model of communication breakdown

them. We advocate for an approach to communication that embraces accountability. Don't blame your failures on a thing that isn't tangible. Be accountable and learn from your errors.

Secret 7: Your Written Messages Are Permanent

As we mentioned earlier, we live in a low-context culture that places a great deal of weight on those things we write. In fact, e-mail has become one of the most preferred channels in the modern workplace because of corporate cultures that value the channel.[25] According to the Pew Internet & American Life Project, e-mail usage has become so commonplace that all four generations in the current workplace have reported usage rates of 90% or greater![26]

Effective business communicators know that the things we put into writing carry legal weight. And as important, the things you put in writing almost never go away entirely. So, you should get into the habit of approaching your written communications from the perspective of the effective business communicator. Treat your written communications as permanent and legally binding.

As of the writing of this book, the 2016 presidential primary season is underway. One problem for Democratic candidate Hillary Clinton is the fact that while acting as secretary of state, she allegedly sent official e-mails using an unsecure, private server and e-mail account. According to some accounts, a number of the e-mails she sent through that server contained national defense information. As a result, she is accused by her political opponents and some in the media of conducting government business via private e-mail and putting national security at risk.[27] Whether this issue goes away or leads to legal problems—as in the case of former CIA Director David Petraeus—remains to be seen. However, a more professional handling of her work communications would have helped her avoid these issues.

In another interesting example of this permanency secret, parents of children attending Brandywine Elementary School were outraged when a satirical form was inadvertently sent with an e-mail advertising events at the school. The bullying report form, titled *Hurt Feelings Report*, mocked children who are victims of bullying and offended many of the families who received the e-mail. Although the school apologized for the error, the e-mail and its ramifications are permanent. The things you put in writing simply don't go away.[28]

Secret 8: Credibility Fuels Communication

How people feel and think about you is largely determined by your credibility, a characteristic comprising trustworthiness and expertise.[29] Think of trustworthiness as the degree to which other people believe that you have their best interests in mind. Expertise has to do with the degree to which people believe you know what you're talking about. Studies show that business professionals with high credibility are better liked and are more persuasive.[30] If you were a financial services customer, wouldn't you rather take advice and purchase products from a professional who is knowledgeable and looks out for your best interest? Effective business communicators understand that credibility is one of the most important factors in shaping their reputations and that they are not naturally endowed with credibility.

Almost anyone in finance would rather do business with Warren Buffet than Tom Hayes. Tom Hayes is a former employee of UBS and Citigroup who is spending 14 years in jail for his role in conspiring to rig the London Interbank Borrowed Rate (LIBOR) interest rate, which is used globally to price financial products. That scandal cost banks billions of dollars to settle with regulators in the United States and Europe.[31] This scandal will cost far more in the long run and will very likely destroy the credibility and careers of some senior banking officials.

Former bank chairman Gianni Zonin is another example of this credibility secret. He was the head of an Italian bank that made it through the most recent recession. The bank was part of the local community. It provided sponsorship to local sports teams and paid for the construction of a theater. But the bank fell on hard times due to bad loans and questions about its business practices. While an investigation is ongoing as of the writing of this book, Mr. Zonin stepped down amid the allegations and his credibility has been destroyed. A recent Morningstar story reported that Mr. Zonin, once a local hero, has become a pariah:

> Mr. Zonin, a 78-year-old wine producer, has gone from respected leader to pariah, banned from a half-dozen restaurants and heckled at his church, residents say. "If I see Mr. Zonin on the street, I take a side street," said Luigi Ugone, a bank shareholder who was recently part of a protest against the bank in the center of Vicenza. "I don't even want to see him."[32]

Credibility is what we in the social sciences call a perceiver construct. In other words, none of us actually has credibility, because it resides in the minds of our audience. We "have" credibility only to the extent that others see us that way. As you've probably heard before, credibility can take a lifetime to build and a minute to destroy. Effective business communicators shape others' perceptions of their credibility by keeping their promises, delivering results for their business partners, communicating in a way that respects others, finding common ground with others, and acting ethically.

Secret 9: Keep It Short

We discussed earlier in this chapter the need to put your audience first. You need to communicate from their perspective. That means you must understand that your audience rarely cares about the same things you do.

Even if they care about the same things, they may not care as deeply as you. Keep your messages clear and short. We have never heard anyone say, "I wish that meeting took up more time." Keep it short.

Secret 10: You Are the Message

Just as important as what you say and how you say it is the fact that you are the one saying it. Effective communicators understand that how the world perceives them has a direct influence on how their behaviors are perceived.[33] In other words, you are the message.

One important takeaway from this secret is that you may not always be the best communicator of your own ideas. Sometimes if you want your idea to be approved or the customer to say yes, then you have to allow someone else to deliver the message. One of our authors—the bald one—holds an administrative position at his university. Faculty members have a natural and healthy skepticism for proposals made by administrators. So, sometimes our bald author will enlist the help of faculty members to make proposals on his behalf. He understands that his messages will be better received by faculty members if they are delivered by faculty members.

You may be familiar with the Volkswagen (VW) emissions scandal that broke in September 2015. A U.S. Environmental Protection Agency investigation concluded that VW installed "defeat devices" on diesel-engined cars. These defeat devices could tell when the cars' emissions were being tested and enhance the cars' performance so that carbon dioxide output would decrease during testing. The findings and eventual admission by VW has led to the recall of millions of vehicles and the company's first quarterly loss in 15 years.[34] A bigger long-term problem may be that VW cannot be taken at its word. Assurances from the company that it will work to fix the problem are being met with harsh skepticism.

Rep. Jan Schakowsky, an Illinois Democrat, said that Volkswagen should buy back the diesel cars at the original purchase price. "If they want it, every VW clean diesel owner should be able to get their money back," she said. … Schakowsky said assurances from the company that the cars will eventually be fixed, perhaps by the end of next year, are not enough. "Volkswagen's word isn't worth a dime," she said. "To find a company that deliberately cheated asking customers for patience, is not acceptable."[35]

Effective business communicators understand that they are their messages. Once your reputation has been tarnished, it is far more difficult to get others to "take your word." Your audience always considers the source.

Conclusion

In this chapter, we hope to have convinced you that following the lessons learned from these ten secrets of effective business communication—summarized in Table 2.1—will help to separate you from the crowd. Many of these lessons are common sense. Despite this fact, too many professionals fail to put the secrets into practice. Being an effective business communicator is hard work. Only those who are willing to put in the effort required to establish and maintain healthy relationships will realize the career-enhancing benefits of the ten secrets.

Table 2.1 Chapter 2 takeaways

Secret	Easy application
Communication = relationships	Deliver bad news without being bad.
People are busy	Respect people's time.
Each communication carries two messages	Pay attention to context.
Nonverbal communication needs to complement verbal communication	Be authentic.
You are not your audience	Put your audience's wants and needs ahead of your own.
Communication breakdown does not exist	Take responsibility for your actions, and learn from your failures.
Your written messages are permanent	Think before you send.
Credibility fuels communication	Keep your promises, deliver results, respect others, find common ground, and act ethically.
Keep it short	Understand that your audience does not care about the same things as you.
You are the message	Act in a way consistent with how you want the world to see you.

CHAPTER 3

Taking Personal Responsibility for Communication Failure

In Chapter 2, we worked to define communication and to share with you some of the secrets that separate the effective business communicators from the rest of us. From our perspective, communication is a process including symbolic, spontaneous, and pseudo-spontaneous messages in which the parties involved are interdependent and able to influence one another. To be effective, we argued that business communicators must (1) get their audience to understand their messages and (2) get their audience to respond appropriately. We also advocated for a personal responsibility approach to business communication.

Remember, there are no breakdowns. As communicators, we sometimes fail to overcome barriers. In this chapter, we discuss the basic communication model and describe common barriers to effective business communication. In addition to describing barriers, we give you the tools to overcome those barriers. Let's begin by taking a look at the basic communication process.

The Communication Process and Personal Responsibility

If you've ever taken a communication course in college, then you've likely seen the process model of communication depicted in Figure 3.1. Although the model offers a relatively simplistic view of a complex process, it also provides you with a starting point when something goes wrong. For example, when you share financial analytics with an audience of non-experts and they give you "trout face" (heads back and mouths open), you can look to the process model to find out what put your audience in that

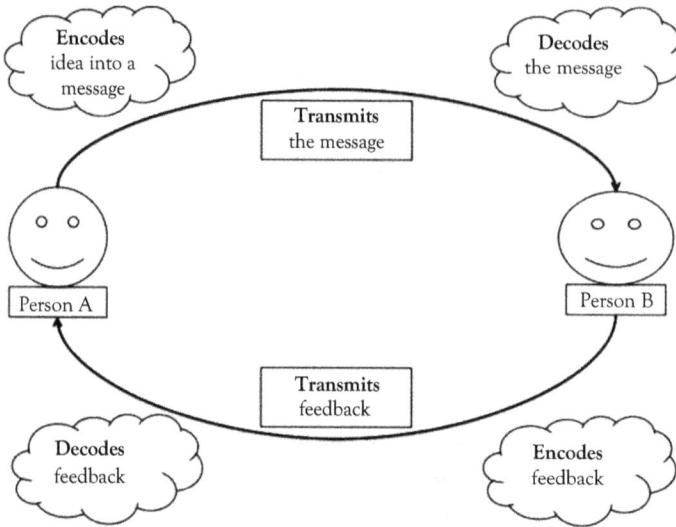

Figure 3.1 Process model of communication

nearly vegetative state. So, let's take a closer look at the process model and what it tells us about barriers to effective communication.

To begin, we should define some of the terms used in the model. In this model, person A begins the communication episode by having an idea and encoding it into a message. Person A transmits the message by some channel (e.g., conversation, e-mail, phone call, text). Person B receives the message, decodes it, and responds in some way. Encoding refers to the process by which we put our ideas into messages using symbols and signs (i.e., words, numbers, expressions, etc.). Decoding is the process by which we assign meaning to symbols and signs. Feedback in this model is simply the response person B has made to person A's message. It's a fairly simple model, but let's take a look at where we can run into barriers that could cause us to be less effective communicators. We can identify places in this model where barriers can impede your ability to communicate. For now, we discuss barriers at the encoding, decoding, and transmitting phases.

Encoding Barriers

The first place where you can encounter barriers is in the encoding phase of the communication process. Barriers at this phase include those things

Box 3.1 Common barriers to encoding

1. Inability to take perspective
2. Lack of knowledge
3. Expertise
4. Emotional interference
5. Limited emotional intelligence
6. Biases
7. Lack of communication skills

that limit your ability to put together a clear, concise message that your audience will understand and respond to appropriately. It is important to remember that our audiences will use whatever information they have available to make inferences about you and your message. Box 3.1 identifies some of the most common barriers to encoding. In this section, we address those barriers.

Inability to Take Perspective

One of the greatest barriers to encoding your messages is the inability to take perspective. As you learned in Chapter 2, you are not your audience. When you fail to consider your audience's perspective, it becomes increasingly difficult to craft messages that speak to their interests, needs, and wants. You should take special care to frame your messages in such a way as to demonstrate that you know your audience's perspective.

We discussed this barrier with Rob Cassella, a financial planner with more than a decade of experience in the finance industry. Over the past six years, Rob has worked for a large financial services firm that offers services such as retirement planning, insurance, financial planning, group retirement, and group insurance. He has a great deal of experience working directly with clients who have little expertise in finance. He told us how important it was for his career to learn how to speak about finance from his clients' perspective. He learned to answer the WIIFM question.

When I first started I really had no idea about "financial talk," if you will. The thing that I learned was that working with clients you need to focus not on the "what" but the "why." So, why are we doing this or why do you have what you have? In other words, what's important to you, the customer? Getting to the core of knowing the client is more important than what it is they have.[1]

Rob Cassela
Financial Planner
Large Financial Services Firm

Lack of Knowledge

Crafting messages that are clear and concise requires that you thoroughly understand the information you're sharing with others. When you write or speak on topics about which you are not well informed, your lack of knowledge becomes evident through inappropriate use of terminology. How can you encode an idea that is accurate and clear if your idea is not well informed?

Expertise

On the other end of the spectrum is what some call the curse of knowledge. Have you ever heard the term *legalese*? It refers to specialized language used by lawyers that most laypeople don't understand. When you have a great deal of knowledge about a very narrow subject, like law or finance, it can be difficult to share that information with people who do not share your knowledge.

Chip and Dan Heath wrote about cursed knowledge in their *New York Times* bestselling book *Made to Stick: Why Some Ideas Survive and Others Die*. What they argue is that once you know something, it becomes difficult to share that knowledge with others because you can't remember what it was like to not know that information. For many of us, it is a challenge to take our audience's perspective (see Barrier #1 and Secret #5 from Chapter 2) and truly appreciate what it means to not have a piece of knowledge. The Heath brothers wrote that "you can't unlearn what you already know. There are, in fact, only two ways to beat the Curse of Knowledge reliably. The first is not to learn anything. The second is to take your ideas and transform them."[2] One way to transform your ideas is to make them simple. Effective business communicators overcome this barrier by developing a keen sense of the language they use, especially in mixed audiences.

We spoke with Eric Bergenn, an assistant branch manager for a full-service financial management company, about some of the boundaries he has confronted in communicating with others. He discussed how challenging it can be to communicate with a lay audience and how important it is to use plain English language.

I find communicating financial information can be most challenging in group settings. I imagine it's a challenge that school teachers and college professors are very familiar with. It's challenging to keep a savvy investor interested while explaining something simple such as compounding returns to someone who has no experience or knowledge. At the same time, it's hard to keep a novice interested while explaining complex retirement income strategies to a savvy investor. I find it's important to avoid industry language and to speak in common terms and analogies when faced with these situations.

I face similar struggles when working internally. People come in to the company with varying levels of understanding, and everyone learns in different ways. What I generally find it to be most important is to use simple, concrete language. There are so many nuances that must be worked on as well for efficiency and to help understanding communicating on a higher level, but a message lost is often of greater value than a nuance gained.[3]

Eric Bergenn
Assistant Branch Manager
Full-Service Financial
Services Firm

Emotional Interference

How you feel affects the way you interact with others. We are all human and we have emotions. Our emotions affect our behavior, including our communication behavior. Emotional displays are not always bad. They do, in fact, demonstrate for others that you are truly invested in what you're discussing. However, emotional outbursts can tarnish your reputation. That's why we always give the advice of "think before you hit send." Effective business communicators understand that they have emotions and work to maintain an awareness of their emotions. They also work to maintain an awareness of others' emotions.

Research has demonstrated that emotions are contagious. Others are influenced by our emotions, and we are influenced by others' emotions.[4] On the positive side, when our enthusiasm for a topic shines through, others are more likely to share in that enthusiasm. To reference the Heath brothers again, one way to enhance the stickiness of our messages is to make our audience feel something. This doesn't mean we manipulate their emotions, but when we demonstrate that we truly care about a topic, others are more likely to care as well.[5]

Unchecked emotions can take away from your key message. For example, a colleague received the message in Box 3.2 from a disgruntled student.

Box 3.2 Emotion-laden e-mail distracting from the message's true purpose

Hi Professor,

I have been trying to get to one of your office hours but i have no time left at work to take to come see you and when i do try to go on my lunch break i always get pulled into having to do something for work or race time in getting my daughter to an appointment. Honesty, I feel so trapped right now. I am ready to give up on school. This being my first semester having a newborn and my boyfriend not helping after my mother law passed away. I feel like I can't have a moment to deal with her passing myself. I haven't slept, I work full time, my mom is sick now, I have to make sure everyone is okay and all I just want to a break. Idk how long I can deal with doing everything by myself. I feel like life is throwing obstacle after obstacle and I am waiting for normal. And a babysitter only comes with cash which i am running low on from having to pay my mom to watch my daughter so i can work. I can't even imagine if i got sick i have no sick time since i went on maternity leave. My daughters father isn't helping he is falling deep into depression and alcohol is his new best friend and i can't even wrap my head around it. I don't sleep because i worry i am going to get a call that he is dead from driving drunk or in the hospital or jail. I wasn't suppose to do this alone i wasn't suppose to have everything fall on me. I don't understand what i have done for him to just run from his responsibilities. I know in a sense he is grieving but i just feel like he is throwing everything away. The plan was for me to stay in school and finish next year but i don't think i can continue because i do not have the time to even get to your work and actual focus on it. For the past couple of weeks i haven't past anything or haven't had the time to contribute to the group discussions. I just stay in my bed at night crying and waiting on the phone that he has gotten home safe not matter how drunk he sounds and by the time i fall asleep i have an hour to wake up for her to feed or for me to go to work. I am trying to stay positive

> but i don't see the positive in any of this. I don't think i will be able to finish school because i don't have enough money to pay for someone to watch my daughter. I don't have enough time to study and when i do sit down to try and understand the work my mind is wondering i can't focus i just want to give up on school and just cry. I never wanted to repeat the cycle of being a single mom but i guess it is happening. I just feel ever day is a test and i am just failing.

The situation the student describes is beyond unfortunate. It's difficult not to feel for her. What does the student want, however, from this professor, beyond empathy? The student cares about school, and you can see that passion, but the emotion has distracted the writer from her goal as a communicator. Moreover, the writer's emotional state has led to a solid block of poorly written text. How might you approach the situation differently?

Limited Emotional Intelligence

Emotional intelligence is a concept that has received greater attention in recent years. According to the work of John Mayer and Peter Salovey, emotional intelligence is "the ability to perceive accurately, appraise, and express emotion; the ability to access and/or generate feelings when they facilitate thought; the ability to understand emotion and emotional knowledge; and the ability to regulate emotions to promote emotional and intellectual growth."[6] People with greater emotional intelligence are more aware of their own emotions and better able to control them. They understand how to display appropriate behavior in any situation.[7] These individuals also have greater social sensitivity and exhibit more prosocial behaviors.[8] These are key factors in communicating goodwill and building meaningful relationships. In fact, some have argued that emotional intelligence has greater impact on career success than cognitive abilities.[9]

Biases

Our biases and stereotypes can influence our ability to put ideas into words. We all hold biases of one sort or another. In particular, the biases you have about the people with whom you are communicating will influence your demeanor and the words you choose. Effective business communicators do their best to understand the biases they hold and to reduce their impact on their messages.

Lack of Communication Skills

Encoding is difficult when you lack the appropriate communication skills to convey ideas to others. Those who do not have adequate speaking, presentation, and writing skills will struggle to achieve the goals of effective business communication. Effective communicators understand that they should always be working to improve their communication skills. You're doing so right now by reading this book.

Decoding Barriers

When you try to place meaning to messages you receive, you can encounter a number of barriers that may prevent you from doing so efficiently. If communication is all about relationships, then both the sender and receiver of messages have some responsibility to overcome communication barriers. Before we dive into specific decoding barriers, you should know that many of the barriers to encoding also affect the decoding process, including the inability to take perspective, lack of knowledge, expertise, emotional interference, and emotional intelligence. In this section, we discuss some of the more common barriers to decoding (see Box 3.3).

Cognitive Schemas and Worldview

Our experiences, both general and specific, lead to the development of our attitudes, values, and beliefs. In turn, these things connect to our

Box 3.3 Common barriers to decoding

1. Cognitive schemas and worldview
2. Attributional biases
3. Information overload and selective perception
4. Listening skills

cognitive schemas. Schemas are how our brain represents and organizes knowledge about people, places, things, and so forth. Our schemas fit together to make up our worldview. Human beings are sense-making creatures. We try to understand the world and integrate our experiences into our worldview. Research tells us that we seek out information that fits and makes sense in our worldview. When we are confronted by information that runs counter to our worldview, we often ignore that information or assimilate it (twist the information to make it fit). The phrase "sit down" can mean any one of a number of things, depending upon your worldview. Is it an invitation to relax? Is it a command from an assertive colleague? How we interpret the phrase will depend upon our worldview. Effective business communicators understand that the way they see the world will influence how they decode information.

Attributional Biases

One of the ways that our worldview can inhibit our ability to process information and decode messages is through attributional biases that we develop. In other words, we try to explain people's behavior. One way we do that is by observing people's behavior over time to look for consistencies. When people behave consistently over time and across situations, we attribute their behavior to a personal characteristic (i.e., personal attribution). When the behavior changes with the situation, we attribute the behavior to the situation (i.e., external attribution). These attributions can lead to errors in how we interpret messages, because our attributions are not always accurate. For example, when someone else takes a loss on an investment, we may attribute it to his or her lack of research or planning. If, however, we experience a great investment loss, we are more likely to contribute it to some feature of the situation beyond our control, such as blaming our investment loss on a tornado that wiped out a company's manufacturing facility.

Information Overload and Selective Perception

Having too much information can make it difficult for us to decode messages. Information overload comes in two forms: quantitative and qualitative. Quantitative overload refers to having too much information. We discussed this idea in Chapter 2. People are busy and are bombarded with messages. Qualitative overload refers to receiving information that is too complex for us to process effectively.

When faced with overload, people choose to pay attention to some information and ignore other pieces of information. Additionally, people often seek affirmation. In other words, they hear what they want to hear and ignore those things that they don't like, can't assimilate, or with which they openly disagree. These selective perception processes can cause us to miss key pieces of information, which results in a lack of understanding.

Listening

We don't listen well. And there are a number of reasons why this is the case. Sometimes we are so excited about making our own point that we simply wait for our turn in a conversation to make our point and forget to listen in the process. Sometimes we use selective perception processes to filter out what we hear. Sometimes we get distracted or use our excess cognitive capacity to think about other things. Sometimes we follow social scripts and simply pretend that we're listening when we are not. We learn the rules associated with listening—we shake our heads at appropriate times or say things like "uh huh" or "I understand" or "I see" in order to move the conversation along, even though we don't actually listen. We hear, but we don't listen.

Listening is not only polite but it's an important way to gain insights into what other people are thinking or what they know. We recently talked with Peter J. Bianco, who has 30 years' experience in banking and owns his own consulting firm that provides analysis of individual commercial loans. He told us about the power of listening skills in his role as a workout officer.

For about 11 years of my banking career, I worked as a workout officer. This involves dealing with commercial loans that have "gone bad." Handling a portfolio such as this involves working with borrowers and business owners who are under a great deal of stress. My primary objective was to do what was best for the bank (i.e., get its money back). When meeting with borrowers, I always made a point to say as little as possible. I would ask pointed questions and listen. On many occasions, I would not speak. This awkward silence always forced the other party to speak ad nauseam. I was able to obtain new and useful information about the situation that would allow me to tailor a solution to the situation and formulate a strategy.[10]

Peter J. Bianco
Managing Member
Consulting Company

Effective communicators understand the importance of truly listening to others, and they use a few simple techniques to help them do so (see Box 3.4).

You can be a better listener during a meeting by taking notes. The simple act of taking notes will help you to focus on what is being said. Provide honest feedback and ask questions. Don't fall back on social

Box 3.4 Tactics to improve your listening skills

1. Take notes
2. Provide honest feedback
3. Ask questions
4. Avoid social scripts
5. Avoid interrupting others
6. Use reflective listening skills

scripts to guide you through the conversation. When all else fails, you can always ask the "who, what, when, where, why, and how" questions. Avoid interrupting people while they are talking. You can also use your reflective listening skills by paraphrasing what you've heard in a meeting or conversation to ensure that you understand.

Transmitting Barriers

The final place where you can encounter barriers in the communication process is at the transmission phase. A number of barriers may confront you at this phase of the process. For now, we focus on two barriers: serial communication chains and channel selection.

Serial Communication Chains

One of the barriers to communicating within and across organizations that you have likely experienced is serial communication chains. Many people are familiar with the grammar school game called "telephone." In it, the first person in the room (usually the teacher) whispers a message to the second person (a student). That student, in turn, whispers the message to the next student, and so on, until the last student hears the message. The last student is then asked to repeat the message for the entire class. What that student says is often vastly different from what the teacher initially said.

Similarly, Jason demonstrates this concept for his students by having one student look at an interesting and complex picture. After a minute of studying the picture, the first student must describe the picture to a second student who has never seen the picture. The second then shares the description with a third student. In this game, the rest of the class takes notes on the mistakes being made in the descriptions. They note what the original observer missed in describing the picture and how the description of the picture changed over time. The results can be fairly alarming to those who care about accuracy.

When information passes serially through a chain, it tends to get warped and distorted. The distortion is usually not intentional. However, each person who receives the message perceives it from a different perspective. The receivers retain the information that fits their worldview, adding or modifying information that doesn't fit, or changing the words in the message. The larger the serial chain, the greater the likelihood that a message traveling through it will be distorted. That's why effective communicators understand that key messages must be delivered directly to the source.

Channel Selection

Another common transmitting barrier is channel selection. Sometimes we send our messages through the wrong channels. Are you a heavy e-mail user? Do you prefer face-to-face meetings? Do you like to make phone calls? Despite what some believe, there is no one best channel for effective communication. The best channel in a given situation depends on its ability to help you achieve the two goals of effective communication: (1) The audience understands the message and (2) responds appropriately.

The channel selections you make can impact how the message is received. Research tells us that the primary motivator behind our selection of communication channel (e-mail, phone, etc.) is our own personal preference.[11] As you learned in Chapter 2, however, your preferences are secondary to your audiences' preferences. Effective communicators try to show sensitivity to their audiences' preferences. They use the channel to which their audience will pay attention. What's the point of leaving a voice mail if the recipient never checks it?

In addition to social information, you have other factors that can help you make the right choice in channel selection. According to the media richness model (see Figure 3.2), you should select the channel for a message based on the match between the channel's richness and the message's equivocality. Equivocality refers to the message's complexity or the number of ways a message can be interpreted. The greater a message's equivocality, the richer the channel needs to be. Richness refers to four factors:

- The degree to which the channel allows for immediate feedback
- The number of cues made available by the channel
- The degree to which the channel allows for the use of natural language

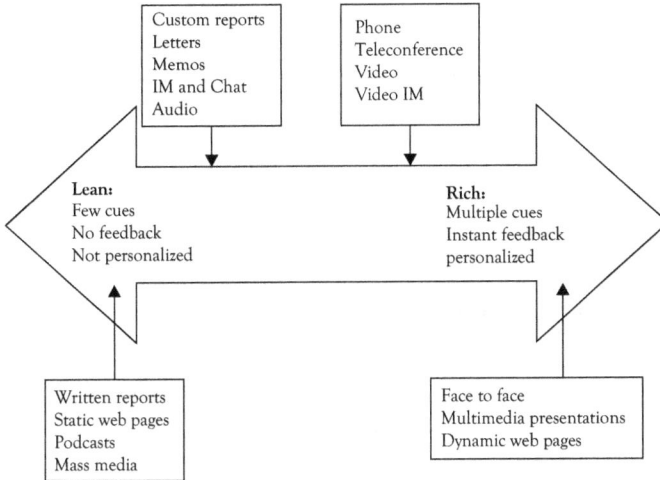

Figure 3.2 Media richness model

- The degree to which the content can be individualized to specific message recipients

Channels such as face-to-face conversations and meetings are rich. Your audience can respond as you speak, all of the verbal and nonverbal cues are available to the audience to aid in interpretation, you can speak naturally, and you can modify the message to fit the specific audience. Channels such as written letters, memos, and e-mails are lean. It takes time for you to receive feedback, many nonverbal cues are unavailable, your business writing is often more formal than your natural language, and it is not possible to adjust the message once it has been sent. According to the media richness model, simple messages can be conveyed by any channel, whereas highly equivocal messages require rich channels.[12] Effective business communicators do their best to match their messages to their channel.

Other Important Barriers

In addition to the barriers we described in the preceding text, you will likely encounter other barriers related to context. In this section, we address two common barriers related to context: culture and gender.

Culture

For our purposes, we consider culture from two perspectives. First, we discuss social cultures, those in which we are raised. Second, we discuss organizational cultures.

Social cultures influence communication behaviors in myriad ways. In a business setting, it is always important to be aware of international customs, lifestyles, politics, and demographics. Cultural awareness will help us avoid ethnocentrism. In addition to these variables, there are four cultural variables that we discuss that may also influence business communication: *individualism-collectivism, time orientation, power distance,* and *context*. It is important to note that we cannot paint people with broad brushstrokes. A person may come from a culture that values individualism, but act in a collectivist manner.

Individualistic societies emphasize independence and reward individual performance. On the other end of the spectrum are collectivist societies, which place groups before people and downplay individual performance. In collectivist cultures, people tend to identify themselves with their social roles and social groups. The dominant culture in the United States is highly individualistic.

Time orientation can vary by social culture. In the United States, we tend to view time as fixed and finite. We schedule meetings and believe that it is rude for people to waste our time, because we have only so much time. Other cultures tend to view time as more fluid and infinite. Those cultures place less emphasis on things like schedules and punctuality.

Power distance refers to the degree to which people accept and respect unequal distribution of power. Cultures with high power distance value authority, hierarchy, and status differences. Cultures with low power distances de-emphasize status differences. The United States is a low power distance culture. It is generally acceptable for people with less status in low power distance cultures to voice objections to their superiors. In his book *Outliers: The Story of Success,* Malcolm Gladwell discussed the impact of power distance on cockpit communications for Korean Air pilots and copilots. He described how the high power distance culture led to copilots and other crewmembers avoiding telling pilots when they were making mistakes. As a result, the airline suffered a number of avoidable accidents before communication training helped to turn things around.[13]

The difference between high- and low-context cultures is the degree of importance that is placed on context, the situational variables that influence an interaction (e.g., gestures, time of day, tone of voice, and social norms). High-context cultures place great emphasis on context in encoding and decoding messages. These cultures hold to the old adage that "it's not what you say, but how you say it that matters." The dominant culture in the United States is low context. Low-context cultures place greater emphasis on what is said or written. That's one reason why we place so much value on things such as contracts in the business world.

Effective communicators understand that it is important to adjust their behavior to meet the needs of the cultural context. We are often asked why we urge our students and clients to adjust their own behavior. There are a few simple answers to that question. First, it is easier to control your own behavior than it is to control others' behavior. Second, as we learned in Chapter 2, communication is an interdependent process. Our behavior will influence others to match our behaviors. Third, the two goals of effective communication require us to always put our audience first.

In addition to social cultures, effective business communicators are sensitive to organizational cultures. Organizations develop their own rituals, languages, values, and worldviews. These cultures can affect how we interact within the organization. For instance, some organizational cultures place great value on competitiveness. In these organizations, employees compete with one another for a fixed pot of rewards. These cultures lend themselves to information hoarding and sabotage. Other organizational cultures emphasize cooperation. Open information sharing is encouraged among employees.

Industries have their own cultures and can develop their own languages. Matthew House is a fixed income analyst and trader who has six years of finance experience with a major investment management group. He recently told us about the industry-specific language learning curve he encountered when he started working on the trading desk as a trading assistant:

I first started working on the desk as a trading assistant and was required to pick up the phone for all incoming calls and relay messages from dealers to the specific sector trader. This was an important part of the training, because every asset class has its own language that needs to be deciphered and understood to make sure you are relaying the correct information. The first few weeks of picking up these calls I felt a major industry specific language barrier. A language of numbers, letters, tickers, spreads, maturities and acronyms all jumbled within short efficient messages for relay. I confronted this barrier by not being afraid to ask questions when I didn't understand something. For example, I would receive a call with the following message:

"15 mm MS 6 1/4 41's at 159, 10 mm CAT 2.6 22's at 64."

That message translates as "Dealer is offering $15 million of the Morgan Stanley 6.25% coupon bonds with a maturity date in 2041 at 159 basis points or 1.59% above the treasury benchmark. Dealer also has $10 million Caterpillar bonds with a 2.6% coupon maturing in 2021 at a spread of 64 basis points above treasury benchmark."

Effective business communicators are not afraid to ask questions to achieve cultural understanding. They are also sensitive to the impact of culture on communications and adjust their behavior accordingly.

Matthew R. House
Fixed Income Analyst and Trader
Investment Management Group

Gender

Despite much uninformed speculation, we do not live in a world of gender inclusiveness. This is just as true in business as many other aspects of life. A 2013 *Harvard Business Review* roundup of research related to gender and work tells the story. First, a McKinsey & Company study revealed that women disappear as you move up the corporate ranks. They account for 53% of entry-level employees, 27% of vice presidents, and only 19% of executives. Those women who leave the workforce are not leaving to care for families but for workplace-related reasons. "High-potential" men receive higher profile assignments with budgets twice as large as their female counterparts. Women in sales make substantially less than their male counterparts. A study of two large stockbrokerage firms found that this was not due to talent differences, but because women were systematically given inferior accounts.[14] As of 2015, the wage gap between men and women who work full-time, year-round jobs stood at just over 78%.

Noted linguist Deborah Tannen has pioneered the research of gender as a cultural variable in business communication. She argues that these noted workplace differences between men and women are due, in part, to differences in communication styles. In particular, her research has found that women tend to share credit more readily, boast less frequently, mitigate criticism with praise, and are less direct and assertive than men.[15] Unfortunately, because men traditionally hold positions of power, the styles of communication more common among women are not valued in the modern workplace. Those in positions of authority tend to assume the logic of their own style and hire and promote people with similar styles. As a result, women may be rewarded less frequently. Effective communicators are sensitive to differences in communication styles and work to make sure that all voices are heard.

Conclusion

In this chapter, we hope to have convinced you to take personal responsibility for your communication behavior (see Box 3.5 for chapter takeaways). The best communicators make mistakes. We all make mistakes. Those of us who are effective learn from our mistakes and do our best to avoid making the same mistakes in the future. Look at communication failures as opportunities for improvement. One way to examine your successes and failures is to look at your behavior through the lens of the communication process model. Be aware of the barriers you will confront and adopt strategies to help you break down those barriers. When you fail to achieve the two goals of effective communication, use the lessons in this chapter to help you make continuous improvements as a communicator.

Box 3.5 Chapter 3 takeaways

1. Effective communication requires that your audience understand your messages and respond appropriately to them.
2. It is your responsibility to understand barriers to communication and work to overcome them.
3. Encoding barriers prevent you from putting your ideas into understandable symbols and signs.
4. Decoding barriers prevent you from adequately understanding information being shared with you.
5. Many of the same barriers can affect both the encoding and decoding processes.
6. Communication channels can cause your messages to become distorted. Choose wisely.
7. Context, including culture and gender, can influence communication processes. Be aware of your own biases and assumptions.
8. You can overcome all barriers to effective communication.

CHAPTER 4

Understanding the Writing Process for Finance Professionals

In Chapter 3, we explored the communication process model to identify common barriers you will confront as business communicators. You were also equipped with the tools to overcome those barriers. In this chapter, we focus our attention on the writing process. Good writers are disciplined and follow a process. We leverage our finance and communication expertise in this chapter to walk you through the writing process and its application to the types of writing activities undertaken in the finance industry. In particular, we introduce you to:

- Using the three "P"s of writing preparation (purpose, people, placement)
- Conducting and incorporating research into your writing
- Proofreading and revising your writing using the four "F" words approach (format, filling, feeling, filth)
- Avoiding common writing errors
- Achieving the ABCs of business writing (accuracy, brevity, clarity)

Using the Three Ps of Writing Preparation: Purpose, People, Placement

So many of the problems that writers face share a common cause: The writer simply did not know what he or she was writing about. We are often so busy and so rushed that we start writing before we've really thought about why we are writing. Think about all of the e-mails you've

Table 4.1 The three "P"s of writing preparation

Purpose	Identify what you want your audience to know, do, or believe as a result of reading your message.
People	Learn what you can about your audience and how that information can influence your style, tone, channel, appeal, and major points.
Placement	Consider the most appropriate organizational pattern for your major points.

written, especially those e-mails that you've written for work. How frequently have you actually stopped and thought critically about the answer to the following question: Why am I preparing this message? The truth is, if you don't ask yourself that question, then you are not likely getting the most out of your messages. If you can't answer that question clearly, then you really have to consider whether you should be writing the message at all. In this section, we talk about a simple method called the three Ps of writing preparation and how this method can make you a remarkably better writer (see Table 4.1).[1]

Purpose

We like to think about message preparation as being similar to the traditional strategic planning process. In that process, the mission statement guides the organization in determining its goals, strategies, and tactics. In other words, the mission statement helps the organization make a series of important strategic decisions that result in the fulfillment of the organization's mission. In mission-driven organizations, tactics are not undertaken if they do not support the mission. Strategic decision making becomes easier. When you are thinking about your message, try to approach the process in a similar fashion. So, you need to start the writing process with a mission statement or purpose statement.

A purpose statement is a sentence that identifies your audience and what you want them to know, do, or believe after reading your message. Before you jump into writing that next e-mail or letter, try to write a purpose statement. As we just said, the purpose statement is not just a couple of words, such as "to convince," "to persuade," "to inform," or "to request." Those expressions are too vague and provide you with little direction.

Consider a typical transmittal document in the finance world, a cover letter accompanying a small business loan proposal. With little thought to the purpose, most people, when asked, might say that the purpose is to get a loan. That purpose would lead to a letter similar to that in Box 4.1. On the surface, the letter appears to be adequate, but with a little more thought about the purpose, you will find that the letter is somewhat incomplete. As we demonstrate in the following text, inadequate attention to the purpose can lead to incomplete documents.

You can easily improve upon this cover letter by asking yourself what you want the reader to know, do, or believe after reading the letter. When considering that question, you will likely come up with an answer such as "I want the lender to review my application materials and contact me to discuss the terms of a loan offer." This purpose reminds you of your audience and what you would like them to do upon reading the letter. It will remind you to consider all of the information you need to provide the reader in order to fulfill your mission, and nothing more.

Box 4.1 Poor loan proposal cover letter

> Dear Ms. Sanchez:
>
> Please review the attached documents related to a loan proposal for On The Treetop, LLC. We are requesting a loan in the amount of $400,000 to expand our operations.
>
> If you have any questions or concerns, please contact me.
>
> Sincerely,
>
> Martin Phelps
> President
> On The Treetop, LLC

In addition to your purpose statement, you should consider the four questions in Box 4.2 that help to clarify your purpose.

These questions help you to consider the secondary objectives for your message. The first question makes you think about the specific and

Box 4.2 Questions that clarify your message's purpose

1. What is it that you really want to achieve with your message?
2. What organizational goals are fulfilled by your message?
3. How can your message support your impression management efforts?
4. How will your message affect key relationships?

immediate actions you want your audience to take. For example, you may want your client to take your advice about how to invest their retirement savings, but what you really want them to do right now is to create a budget to increase savings by $1,000 per month to direct toward a 401(k) plan. The second question is important, especially for internal communications. If you can tie your message to an important organizational goal, then people are more likely to respond. The third question is a simple reminder to consider how you'd like people to see you. Does your message accomplish that objective? The final question asks you to think carefully about how your message affects other people.

Let's apply the questions in Box 4.2 to the purpose statement we provided to you for the cover letter accompanying a small business loan proposal. The purpose statement directly responds to Question 1. The purpose does not really address Question 2. The lender who reads the letter will want to know what's compelling about your plans to use the loan. The supporting documents accompanying the cover letter will provide details about what you will do with the funds from a loan, but the cover letter should pique the lender's curiosity. Question 3 addresses the impression you want to make in the cover letter. Because your credibility is so important in a letter of this type, you will want to strike a more formal tone than usual. You will also need to demonstrate that you've done your homework and thought thoroughly about the proposal process. Finally, Question 4 serves as a reminder to you that this is an opportunity to build a new business relationship or maintain an existing relationship.

In many cases, thinking your way through a clear purpose and the four questions in Box 4.2 will take a few moments, but those few moments will result in better communication. With careful consideration of the purpose, the cover letter can be improved and look like the one in Box 4.3.

Box 4.3 Improved loan proposal cover letter

Dear Ms. Sanchez:

In 2014, I started On The Treetop, LLC, a small business that designs children's clothing. The business has flourished so significantly that I need to expand to keep up with demand. This expansion requires an investment. Therefore, I am requesting that you review the attached supporting documents and contact me concerning my proposal for a loan in the amount of $400,000.

Attached are the following documents to support my loan proposal:

Executive summary	Business summary	Management resumes
Business plan	Financial statements	Financial projections
Marketing plan	Loan application	Repayment plan and collateral
Business credit report	Income tax returns	

You will see that our market research has uncovered a strong and growing market for the type of children's clothing made by On The Treetop. We project the market to continue to expand for the next 15 years. A loan of $400,000 would allow On The Treetop to capitalize on this opportunity by

- Renting a location that will serve as both factory and storefront
- Purchasing advertising
- Expanding into the mail order market
- Increasing local market share

I am sure you will find I have an excellent credit history and a solid business plan. Please let me know if you have any questions or require any further documentation. I am looking forward to the opportunity to talk with you more about the attached loan proposal.

Sincerely,

Martin Phelps
President
On The Treetop, LLC

You may be saying to yourself, "The improved letter is longer than the poorly written letter. I thought you said shorter was better." We do believe you should be as concise as possible. However, in being concise, you must still accomplish your goals as a writer. Therefore, shorter notes are not always better if they leave out important information and fail to achieve your strategic purpose.

People

As we've mentioned repeatedly, you will want to know as much about your audience as possible. You need to be able to answer the WIIFM question and know how the reader might react to your message. Being able to predict their reaction will help you determine how you will organize the information in your message (see section "Placement" in the following text). Knowledge of your audience will also help you make important strategic choices, such as the degree of formality you should achieve in your writing, the language you use, and the channel you select for sending your message. It's also important to consider secondary audiences and not alienating them.

When planning your messages, consider the tactics in Box 4.4 to help you build messages that suit your audience.

Think about the language you will use and how it will set your audience's frame of mind. Use plain language with familiar words, which shows your audience you can speak their language and have common ground. Be courteous and positive. Try to highlight positive information, without obscuring reality. We all have to deliver bad news, such as telling a customer that he or she is being denied credit. Being sensitive to how we deliver that news is important. Instead of writing something like

---

Box 4.4 Planning a message that suits your audience

1. Cultivate a "you" view
2. Use conversational language
3. Use positive language
4. Use plain English
5. Be courteous
6. Highlight audience benefits

"Your credit application has been rejected," you can say, "We are unable to extend credit to you at this time."

Cultivating a "you" view means that you typically want to keep the focus on your audience. Audiences care about themselves before anything else, and people see the world from their own perspective. So, instead of writing something like "I am sending the February sales data report to you tomorrow," write, "You can expect to receive the February sales data report from me by tomorrow." And finally, before writing your messages, think about how your audience will benefit from adopting your ideas or following your advice. Focus on audience benefits, not the features of your ideas.

Placement

In addition to thinking about purpose and people, you should also consider the placement of content in your message. In other words, how will you organize your message, given your purpose and audience(s)? In this section, we offer tips for placing your content in such a way as to have a maximum impact on your audience.

For our students at Central Connecticut State University, we recently developed a business-writing guide called the CCSU Guide to Writing. The guide is meant to help students think critically about the content they will need produce when writing business messages. The CCSU Guide to Writing (see Box 4.5) can be adapted to meet the needs of myriad business-writing situations, such as informative e-mails, memos, business plans, and analytical reports. We hope the guide will also help you think through your approach to writing.

Box 4.5 The CCSU writing guide

Communicate the issue(s) or problem(s)

Clarify your approach to the issue(s) or problem(s)

Scrutinize your approach

Utilize your approach to resolve the issue(s) or solve the problem(s)

First, your messages will need to communicate the issue(s) or problem(s) being addressed in the message. When you communicate the issue(s) or problem(s) to your audience, you will need to consider their perspective. What do they know? What do they need to know? Provide your audience with the information necessary to understand the situation and the key issue(s) or problem(s) that will be addressed in your message. This vital background information will create context for your audience and set the appropriate frame of mind.

In addition to communicating the issue(s) or problem(s), you will also need to clarify your approach to the issue(s) or problem(s). You can approach any issue or problem from a number of different angles, using different theories, models, or philosophical approaches. You should clarify your approach for the reader. This means that you will have to discuss why the approach is most suitable to the situation and what about the situation makes your approach the best. You may also have to acknowledge other approaches and contrast them to your own. The less your audience knows about your approach, the more detail you will need to provide.

You should be your own best critic. Scrutinize your approach; put it to the test. Run the variables of the situation through your chosen approach (e.g., best and worst case scenarios). Analyze available data and information using your approach. Describe the outcomes to your audience, using examples when possible.

Finally, most business-writing situations are persuasive in nature and require you to offer resolutions to issue(s) or solutions to problem(s). Make actionable recommendations, whenever possible. Describe what the reader should do, justify the recommendation(s), provide an implementation plan, and suggest how success can be assessed.

Placement for Approach

The CCSU Guide to Writing will help you think through the information you will need to present to your audience. The placement of information in a message depends on whether you plan to use a direct or an indirect approach (see Table 4.2).

In business, audiences tend to prefer a direct approach. A direct approach requires the writer to state the main idea(s) early in the message,

Table 4.2 Situations for using direct and indirect approaches

Direct approach	Indirect approach
Delivering good news	Delivering bad news
Engagement letter	Investor proposal letter—new product
Request for proposal	Explaining reduction in dividends
Price quotes	Credit denials

followed by relevant information or details or both. However, it will sometimes benefit you and your message to use an indirect approach. In an indirect approach, you provide the relevant information or details or both first, followed by the message's main idea(s).

How do you know when an indirect approach is appropriate? The best way to be able to answer that question is to know the first two Ps: purpose and people. When you need to provide routine information; share good news; or ask your audience to take action that they are willing to take, use a direct approach. When you need to share bad news; overcome audience disagreements; or ask your audience to take action that they will likely resist, you should use an indirect approach. In other words, you need to gauge your audience's reaction to the message to determine which approach is most appropriate. So, now you may be asking why an indirect approach is best when the message elicits a negative response from the audience. The indirect approach works best in these situations for a couple of reasons.

First, if you know the information you are sharing will cause distress for your audience, then an indirect approach will give you the chance to soften the impact of negative information. If you have ever received a loan denial letter, you will have noticed that it likely started with a phrase, such as "Thank you for your contacting us to discuss available loan options. We understand that this may come at a difficult time, however based on careful review of the information provided ...." Most people understand that if the message doesn't open with "congratulations," then they were likely rejected. Using a buffer in an indirect approach gives the reader time to come to terms with the conclusion before actually reading it.

Second, persuasion attempts that are likely to be met with resistance use an indirect approach because of selective perception processes. We know that people will disregard information that runs counter to their own ideas. In some cases, your audience will begin to refute your argument once they know you're going to ask them to do something they don't want to do. If you were going to ask a department manager to slash his or her workforce by 10%, you would not want to open the message with that statement. That manager will either shut down mentally and not listen to the rationale or will counter argue with the rationale. By providing the rationale before making your request, you increase the odds that the audience will at least listen to the argument.

Placement for Memory

In addition to thinking about using a direct or indirect approach, you should also think about placing information within a document in a way that makes it easy for your audience to remember. Here are some tactics you can employ to make your supporting points easier to remember.

Not all supporting points in a document are created equally. Some of your arguments will have greater impact on your audience than others. Therefore, you should take advantage of the primacy–recency effect, which suggests that people tend to best remember information that they see first or last. Your most impactful supporting points should be placed either near the beginning of your message or near the end of the message. Avoid burying your best supporting points in the middle of the message.

When you provide your readers with a long list of details or many key pieces of information, try to find natural ways to organize that information and make an effort to present the information in those natural categories.[2] These "chunks" of information are easier for our audience to remember.[3] Consider the vague assortment of information presented in Table 4.3.

Now consider the information in Table 4.3 and compare it to Table 4.4. Which of those two lists is easier to memorize?

The list in Table 4.4 should be easier to memorize. The information is organized into four categories. This simple act of organizing information makes it not only easier to memorize but also easier to lock away into your long-term memory. Try to apply this idea into your communications. Your audience will retain the information and be better able to recall it later when they need it.

Table 4.3 Unorganized pieces of information

Adidas	Bond
Adventure	Fifteen
Puma	Deposit
Credit	Asics
Horror	Seventy
Eight	Collateral
Debit	Comedy
Fantasy	Drama
Thirteen	Nike
Reebok	Forty

Table 4.4 Chunked pieces of information

Popular shoe brands	Numbers
Reebok	Eight
Adidas	Forty
Puma	Fifteen
Asics	Seventy
Nike	Thirteen
Common banking terms	**Movie genres**
Bond	Fantasy
Collateral	Comedy
Credit	Horror
Debit	Adventure
Deposit	Drama

Conducting Research for Writing in Finance

There may be times when finance professionals are required or need to conduct research in order to become more knowledgeable on a topic for a report, for a client, or to improve the depth of their knowledge in a particular area. In academic research, we start the research process by choosing a topic that interests us; in the real world of business, however, the topic will generally present itself. For example, a company CEO asks a financial analyst to determine if a target business is a worthwhile investment.

Before diving into research, it's important to go through some simple preparatory exercises to ensure that the research process is efficient and effective. We provide a summary review of the research process's eight important elements. For a detailed exposition of business research and methodology, we recommend *Essentials of Business Research: A Guide to Doing Your Research Project* by Jonathan Wilson.

1. ***Create a list of key search terms.*** Brainstorm search terms or key words that will help to research the topic. If you don't know anything about the topic, it may be helpful to conduct a cursory search via a search engine to at least have an idea of where to begin.

2. ***Write a goal or purpose statement.*** What exactly is it you need to discover by researching this topic? The statement should be detailed enough to guide your research. For example, our financial analyst may ask if investing in the target business will provide a rate of return greater than the required return.

3. ***Develop questions to guide the search.*** What questions do you have about the topic? Use the purpose statement to guide your thought process. Group questions into subtopics, if warranted. These subtopics may become headings in the finished research report. Expanding upon the example of researching a target business, our financial analyst may ask: What drives company revenue? What do you need to know about the business, the business strategy, and how the management runs it? What do you need to know about the industry within which the company operates? What is the company's competitive position? Has there been any suspicious activity on the financial statements? Have there been large changes in assets or liabilities? What are the company's financial ratios? How do the financial ratios compare to those of other companies in the same industry? How have the financial ratios changed over time?

4. ***List potential sources.*** Make a list of sources that you can use to research the topic. These may include websites, books, journals, databases, and other sources that are company provided, publicly available online, or available at libraries. For example, our financial analyst may seek out financial reports at the Securities and Exchange Commission (SEC) EDGAR database, industry reports at Hoovers,

and materials available from investor days and investor conference call transcripts at the company investor relations website. A thorough researcher will seek out sources of information that others may not have considered.

5. *Take thorough notes during research.* Create a document within which to take notes for each source being utilized in the search. Use your purpose statement and prepared questions to guide you in searching each source. Keep thorough notes on search terms used and locations searched in case you need to return to a search. Thorough notes will also make the research process more efficient, eliminating repetition of the same search and providing a clear path to follow when documenting the research process and creating citations and references.

6. *Gather data, if necessary.* In most finance research, statements or ideas may require data-driven research and thus need to be supported with statistics. Data may be collected manually by the researcher, for example, from company annual reports or from online providers such as Google Finance. Some data may be published and either publicly available or available for purchase from data providers, for example, government-provided census data and SEC filings, or Standard & Poor's.

7. *Develop the thesis.* Once you have completed enough research on the topic, the purpose statement can be strengthened into a thesis statement, which is written from the researcher's point of view and can be strongly supported by the research. In our case, it may be that the target business is not a worthwhile investment because the estimated return on investment is less than the required return.

8. *Write the report.* Using your questions or subtopics, create an outline for your report and write the body of the report. The body proves your thesis statement using the notes you captured from researching each of the sources. Ensure sources are properly cited as you work. Finally, write the introduction, which should include the first statement of the thesis, and a conclusion including a restatement of the thesis and a summary of the main points. Include a list of references, ensuring all works cited are included and properly referenced. Proofread your work, and enlist a colleague or friend to proofread for you.

Proofreading and Revising Using the Four F Words

Jason created the four F words approach a few years ago to help his students develop a disciplined approach to proofreading and revising (see Figure 4.1).[4] The four F words process takes you through four steps that focus the writer's attention on increasing levels of detail. Even with the four F words process, you will still occasionally make mistakes that go unnoticed. After all, nobody is perfect. The process will, however, help you avoid becoming the person from whom writing mistakes are expected frequently. The four F words of proofreading and revising will help you produce clean documents and maintain your professional reputation.

Format

The first F word asks you to take a big picture look at your document. You are asking yourself if the document looks the way it is supposed to look. Assess the document's formatting. In doing so, you can ask a few simple questions to guide you through this step in the process.

Does the Document Meet Your Organization's Standards?

Many companies have standards for how documents should look. They often offer templates and guides to reinforce the company's brand image through a consistent appearance. Before anything else, you should make sure that you're following your organization's standards for document design.

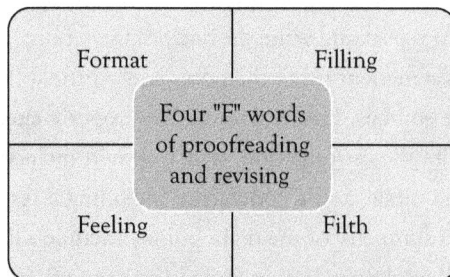

Figure 4.1 The four "F" words of proofreading and revising

Do the Key Ideas Jump Off the Page?

Most readers first approach a document by skimming it. We are all so busy that we try to quickly find the information that matters to us. To help readers find important points, use mechanical devices that cause the ideas to jump off the page. For example, we can write important ideas in **bold**, *italic,* underlined, or ***a combination*** of font styles. In addition, you can use one or more of the following (but be careful not to overuse):

- Bulleted and enumerated lists
- Color
- Tables and figures
- ALL CAPS
- Headings and subheadings

Is the Document Readable?

Readability refers to how easily a message can be read and understood. One of the easiest ways to enhance a document's readability is to avoid what we call the WALL OF WORDS effect. You are familiar with wall of words documents; they are the documents that have long sentences, long paragraphs, and use full justification. These documents are difficult to skim because the text runs from the left margin of the page to the right margin with little use of white space. A busy reader may jump to the next document rather than spend the time trying to break through the wall of words.

Filling

In Step 2 of the process, you can move beyond the document's appearance and begin looking at the content. You are trying to determine if, given your purpose, the content is adequate. We have provided you with a few questions to help guide you through Step 2 of the process.

Is the Purpose Clear?

We discussed the importance of your purpose statement earlier in this chapter. We hope that you always develop a clear purpose before you begin the writing process. However, it is a good idea to check your purpose to make sure it is clear. If your purpose is not clear to you, how will it be clear to the reader?

Is All Necessary Information Included and Organized?

Answering this question effectively requires that you first have a few key pieces of information yourself. First, you need to have sufficient content knowledge about the message's topic. Do your research. Make sure you have collected information from credible sources and that you have both quantitative and qualitative information. When you make claims, you will need the evidence to support them.

In addition to sufficient content knowledge, you also need to understand your audience thoroughly. You need to determine what information they have and what information they need, the questions they may ask, and the emotional response they will have to the information. Try to answer the WIIFM question. To be convincing, you also need to understand what forces will move your audience to say yes to your requests and what forces are holding them back from saying yes. To be most effective, you will need to make sure your content is appropriate for your audience.

Feeling

It is important that you make sure that your messages demonstrate respect for your audience and strike the appropriate tone. Your audience will evaluate your professional image based, in part, on the messages you write. In this step of the process, you are trying to be a collegial professional and a good steward of your professional image. To guide you through Step 3 of the process, try to answer the following questions.

Do You Make Polite Requests?

Just because you may find yourself in a position of authority does not mean that manners don't matter. Even when making directives, please remember that you are asking people to complete tasks. Use of "please" and "thank you" will serve you well throughout your career. For example, consider the difference between the following two sentences:

- *You must have the report to me* by 8 a.m. tomorrow.
- *Please complete the report* by 8 a.m. tomorrow.

Both sentences include a request for action. In both cases, you can expect the report by 8 a.m. However, the second sentence demonstrates more respect for the audience by using "please." As the expression goes, you can catch more flies with honey.

Do You Avoid Abstract Words and Phrases?

We have made the point more than once about the importance of using language that your audience understands. Not only is it important to help your audience better understand the information you are sharing, but considering your use of language is also a matter of respect. It is disrespectful to use language that your audience will not understand.

Are Your Emotions in Check?

When we allow our emotions to dictate what we write, we often win short-term emotional boosts at the expense of fulfilling our document's true purpose. Do your best to keep your purpose in mind and moderate your emotions.

Do You Make the Effort to Soften the Blow of Bad News?

As you will see in Chapter 5, you will be called upon to write bad news messages. You will find yourself in positions where you must say no to requests, fire employees, deny promotions, cut relations with vendors, deny customer claims, and write many other uncomfortable messages. Please remember that how you handle such situations can have lasting consequences. Do your best to be considerate of your audience's feelings when delivering bad news.

Filth

Now that you know the document looks right, has the appropriate content, and treats your audience with respect, you can take a look at spelling, grammar, and mechanics. These errors are like little pieces of filth that are detrimental to your document's clarity and your reputation.

Use Word Processing Power

When using word processing programs, you have certainly encountered those red and green squiggly lines underneath your sentences that indicate an error of some type. You should always stop and review those sentences. However, use your brainpower to determine if an error actually exists. Avoid blindly accepting changes that the program suggests. Word processing programs are not written by professional copy editors. As a result, these programs occasionally identify nonexistent problems (i.e., cry wolf), fail to identify real problems (i.e., miss the boat), and offer incorrect solutions to real problems. Word processing programs are amazing little tools, but like all tools, we must engage our brain while using them or suffer the consequences.

Change the Medium

Finding our own errors is not easy to do. Just because you produce a document using a program such as Microsoft Word doesn't mean that you must proofread it using that software or using a computer screen. Try printing out important documents and reviewing them on paper. Changing the medium slows down our brains a little.

Trick Yourself

Another reason why we often miss our own errors is that we don't expect to see them. When you draft a document, you think about what you want to write before you actually write it down. How often does the version in your mind have errors? Based on the ideas of selective perception, if you don't expect to see errors, you won't. One thing you can do to trick yourself and work against selective perception is to proofread your documents from the last line to the first. Start at the end and work to the beginning.

Read Aloud

Another way to slow down your brain is to read your messages aloud. You read aloud at a slower rate than you read quietly to yourself. Reading aloud helps you find small errors in spelling, grammar, and mechanics because you will likely stumble in places where errors exist. This tip also helps you make sure you've struck the appropriate tone.

The ABCs of Writing: Accuracy, Brevity, Clarity

While making your final revisions, please remember that your goal is to achieve the ABCs of writing. Your messages need to be accurate, brief, and clear. Often, the pieces of filth that we are looking to eliminate in Step 4 of the proofreading and revising process work against the ABCs of writing. In this final section of the chapter, we share with you some ideas that will help make your writing accurate, brief, and clear. Because this book is meant to be a brief guide, we do not provide you with an exhaustive list, just those ideas that you can easily put into practice today. For a more complete treatment of writing, we recommend the following supplementary resources:

- *The Elements of Style* by William Strunk Jr. and E.B. White. This book is a must-have resource for any professional who takes writing seriously. It provides the basic rules for writing in the plain English style. And, according to the authors, "It concentrates on fundamentals: the rules of usage and principles of composition most commonly violated."[5] Jason has owned his copy of the book since 1997 and always keeps it handy. You should do the same. In fact, you can download a PDF copy of the book from www.goodreads.com.
- *HBR Guide to Better Business Writing* by Bryan A. Gardner. This book represents a more modern take on writing and focuses exclusively on business writing. The appendixes are particularly useful as they contain essential grammar rules, punctuation rules, and business-writing etiquette guidelines.[6]

- *Purdue Online Writing Lab (OWL).* This site offers comprehensive advice on all things related to writing. In particular, we recommend brushing up on your basic writing skills by using the OWL Exercises, which include exercises on grammar, punctuation, spelling, sentence structure, sentence style, and number writing. At https://owl.english.purdue.edu/exercises/ you can find the exercises online
- *Wisconsin University-Madison Writing Center.* This writing center, like many others, offers advice on avoiding 12 common writing errors and provides useful assistance. It covers topics such as parallelism and dangling or misplaced modifiers. You can find the guide and download it from the following website: http://writing.wisc.edu/Handbook/CommonErrors.html

Common Errors That Work Against the ABCs

Errors in punctuation and grammar usage can slow down your reader and cause confusion in interpretation. Let's examine some common culprits.

Misuse of Apostrophes

Paul Simon's song "American Tune" opens with the following: "Many is the time I've been mistaken and many times confused. Yes, and I've often felt forsaken and certainly misused." We can't help but wonder if that isn't how the apostrophe feels. Writers frequently misuse apostrophes when they write possessives and contractions. Possessives and contractions are very different things, and we hope to help you avoid the confusion.

Why do people confuse possessives and contractions? They both frequently use apostrophes. For example, in the phrase *Helen's price quote,* the word "Helen's" is a possessive that needs an apostrophe. But possessives don't always require an apostrophe. In the phrase, *Your time is important,* the word "your" is a possessive that does not require an apostrophe. Notice that we used the possessive "your" and not the contraction "you're." Contractions are shortened versions of words or word groups. In this case, "you're" is short for "you are."

Table 4.5 Guidelines for appropriate use of apostrophes

Rule	Example
Use apostrophe + s when the possessive noun is singular and does not end in "s."	*Helen's price quote*
Use apostrophe after the "s" when the possessive noun is plural and ends in "s."	*The advisors' suggestions*
Use apostrophe + s when the possessive noun is singular, ends in "s," and can be pronounced after you add apostrophe + s.	*Mr. Jones's third-quarter estimates*

Similarly, people frequently misuse the possessive "its" and the contraction "it's." So, how can you be sure if you're using contractions such as "it's" correctly? The best answer is to read the sentence aloud with the full word or word groups that are contracted by the apostrophe. If the words "it is" do not sound right in the sentence, then you probably don't need a contraction. You probably need the possessive form "its." For another example, consider the expression, *You'll see that our market research has uncovered a strong and growing market.* Expand the contraction "you'll" with the words "you will" and read the sentence aloud. It sounds right because it is right. This sentence needs a contraction, not a possessive. The apostrophe is in the appropriate place.

The poor apostrophe is commonly misused in another way. It is frequently put in the wrong place when used with a possessive noun. We are frequently asked if the apostrophe goes before or after the letter "s." That's a simple question with a simple answer. Unfortunately, many people use the wrong rule to derive the answer. They believe that if the possessive noun is plural, then the apostrophe follows the "s," and if the possessive noun is singular, the apostrophe precedes the "s." That rule is false. To help you use the apostrophe appropriately, follow the guidelines in Table 4.5.

Errors in Subject–Verb Agreement

A subject and its verb must both be either singular or plural. Although seemingly simple, this rule is difficult to follow because it is easy for us to get tricked. Compound subjects trick even the best writers. Compound subjects combine two subjects with the word "and." When the two subjects represent one singular idea, the compound subject is singular. For example, Grammar Girl (another great online resource) notes that "peanut butter and jelly" is a singular compound subject because it is one dish. So, that compound subject should be paired with a singular verb. Let's see that expression in action:

- Peanut butter and jelly is my favorite treat.

The compound subject "peanut butter and potatoes" is plural. The two foods are not one treat. They are two separate treats. Therefore, they should be paired with a plural verb, as in the following expression:

- Peanut butter and potatoes are my favorite treats.[7]

Sentences starting with "there" can cause good writers to pair the subject with the wrong verb tense. Bryan Garner argued that people tend to use singular verbs with "there" regardless of the sentence's true subject. In his book, he used the following example: *There is still market capacity and established competition to be considered.* In this expression, the compound subject "capacity and competition" should be paired with the plural verb "are." In these cases, we suggest an alternative solution. Do your best to avoid sentences that start with "there." The expression in the preceding text could be written in the following way: *Market capacity and established competition are still to be considered.*

Errors in Hyphen Use

Use hyphens to combine compound modifiers, which are two words that act as one adjective and clarify the meaning of a noun. For example, in the expression *five-year contract*, the words "five" and "year" are modifiers of the word "contract." Notice that a compound modifier is two words. Therefore, an expression such as *nonbinding arbitration* does not require a hyphen because "non" is a prefix, not a word. The same is true for other prefixes such as pre, ante, infra, pro, over, and post. The rule for hyphen use has an exception. Avoid using a hyphen when the compound modifier includes an adverb ending in –ly, such as *newly minted PhD.*

Errors in Number Use

The rules for number use in business are not so clear. However, you can avoid most egregious errors by following the guides we offer in Table 4.6.

In addition to the guides offered in Table 4.6, you should aim for internal consistency with your number use. In other words, use numbers consistently within a sentence. For example, in the expression *We need 20 investors in 3 days,* because the writer used the figure for 20, he or she also used the figure for 3.

Table 4.6 Guidelines for using numbers correctly

General use: Write numbers one through ten as words, write numbers above ten as figures, and write all numbers as words if they appear at the beginning of a sentence.	
Wrong	**Correct**
We have 1 more day.	We have one more day.
We have twenty more days.	We have 20 more days.
20 days remain until the opening.	Twenty days remain until the opening.
Money and dates: Write sums greater than $1 as figures, write numbers in dates as figures if the day appears after the month, and write numbers in dates as ordinals if the day appears before the month.	
Wrong	**Correct**
He invested fifteen million dollars.	He invested $15 million.
The loan payment is due on June fifth.	The loan payment is due on June 5.
The loan payment is due on June 5th.	The loan payment is due on the 5th of June. The loan payment is due on June 5.
Clock time: Write numbers as figures when expressed with a.m. or p.m., drop the colon and last two digits when referring to the top of the hour, and write numbers as words when written with the word "o'clock."	
Wrong	**Correct**
five p.m.	5 p.m.
5:00 p.m.	5 p.m.
5 o'clock	five o'clock

Errors in Capitalization

Writers commonly capitalize words that should not be capitalized, and they fail to capitalize words that require a capital letter. Here are some guidelines that will help you avoid those errors.

- Capitalize proper nouns (e.g., Canada).
- Capitalize titles when they precede the person's name (e.g., President Miller).
- Do not capitalize titles when it follows the person's name (e.g., Mr. Miller, president) or when it is not associated with a person's name (e.g., president).

Errors in Use of Semicolons and Commas

Semicolons and commas are hard to work with. Here's a simple guide for using semicolons. In sentences, semicolons are used to separate two independent clauses that have been combined to make a single sentence. For example, consider the following sentence:

My intern had a problem; he had to find his TPS report quickly.

Both the first clause (my intern had a problem) and the second clause (he had to find his TPS report quickly) are independent clauses. You would not separate those two clauses with a comma. In fact, if you separate two independent clauses with a comma, you are committing a style error called a comma splice. So, when do you use commas in sentences?

First, you can combine two independent clauses with a comma if you add a coordinating conjunction (e.g., and, but, or) after the comma. But in order to fix a comma splice this way, it must make sense for the two independent clauses to be joined by a coordinating conjunction. It does not make sense to combine the aforementioned clauses about the intern and his TPS report with a comma and coordinating conjunction. You could, however, use a comma and coordinating conjunction in the following example:

My intern had a problem, but he still had time to find his TPS report.

Second, use commas after an introductory clause such as in the following sentence:

If you have ever been to a conference, you probably worked hard to meet new people.

The first clause (if you have ever been to a conference) is dependent. That means it needs the second clause in order to be a complete sentence. A comma is needed to combine the two clauses.

Third, use commas to separate out a clause in the sentence, which is not central to the meaning of the sentence. For example, consider the following sentence:

We should host the conference on June 14, Flag Day, because our venue of choice is available.

The fact that June 14 is Flag Day is not central to the meaning of the sentence and is set off by commas.

Finally, use commas when words are repeated, such as in the following sentence:

I am very, very happy to see you.

You should also use a comma when two coordinate adjectives are used to describe a noun, such as in the following sentence:

She wrote a series of timely, insightful recommendations.

Using Dangling and Misplaced Modifiers

Modifiers add description to other words in a sentence. A misplaced modifier is simply a word that is separated from the word it modifies. A modifier dangles when the word it modifies is not clearly stated in the sentence. When they are misplaced or dangling, modifiers can reduce a sentence's clarity. We find that our students are unfamiliar with dangling and misplaced modifiers, but they understand them once they see a couple of examples. So, let's take a look at the following example:

After leaving the meeting, the report's recommendations started to make sense to her.

In this example, the modifier is misplaced. The introductory clause "after leaving the meeting," is a modifier. What word does it modify? The sentence as written suggests that the report's recommendations left the meeting. When an introductory clause serves as a modifier, the noun being modified should be the first noun following the clause. In other words, you can always ask "who or what" after the introductory clause. In this case, you can ask, "Who or what left the meeting?" The answer to that question should be the next noun you see in the sentence. The woman left the meeting, not the report's recommendations. Therefore, we need to fix the sentence. Here is one way that it can be fixed.

After leaving the meeting, she started to make sense of the report's recommendations.

Now let's take the same example and commit a dangling modifier error. If we wrote the sentence in the following way, it would be a dangling modifier because the word being modified is not clearly stated.

After leaving the meeting, the report's recommendations started to make sense.

Not only is the modifier "after leaving the meeting" misplaced, it is also dangling because the woman who left the meeting is not mentioned. We can fix the dangling modifier the same way we fixed the misplaced modifier.

After leaving the meeting, she started to make sense of the report's recommendations.

Using Passive Voice Without a Subject

Passive voice sentences lack clarity and are often longer and less direct than active voice sentences. Passive voice sentences follow the object–verb–subject pattern, and they occasionally omit the subject. Active voice is preferred because it tends to be more direct and clearer. The following sentences both have "Fran" as the subject and "the transaction" as the object. The first sentence is in active voice and the second sentence is in passive voice.

Active: Fran committed an error in processing the transaction.

Passive: An error in processing the transaction was committed by Fran.

Many writing pundits will tell you that the active voice is almost always preferred. Others, however, will argue that both sentences are clear about who committed the error. The problem with passive voice in business writing is really about identifying the subject. If an error was committed, the reader will want to know who committed the error. Consider the same sentence in passive voice without the subject.

Passive and no subject: An error in processing the transaction was committed.

Those who give you the advice to avoid passive voice want to make sure that the subject is always clear. The reader should know who is doing what. Business writers who want to be clear will use active voice because it tends to use fewer words. When they use passive voice, they work hard to ensure the subject is clear.

Avoid It Is or Was and There Is or Are Starters

One easy way to be more concise in your writing is to look for sentences that begin with some variation of "it is" or "there are." When you see those two words, they can be deleted. With some minor changes, which usually include the deletion of a pronoun or relative pronoun, your sentences will be shorter without sacrificing clarity. Look at the following example of a sentence with a "there are" starter.

There are many factors that have contributed to our firm's recent successes.

The sentence could be shorter and the first thing you can do is eliminate the words "there are." You can also delete the relative pronoun "that." You are left with the following shorter sentence.

Many factors have contributed to our firm's recent successes.

You may be asking why eliminating a few words should matter so much. As we've discussed earlier, it's important to appreciate people's time. You should also think about the costs associated with the words you use. Every word costs time and money. Small changes over the course of a lifetime can result in large savings.

Avoid Flabby Expressions

Business writers sometimes fall into the trap of using expressions that are needlessly long. Writers do this because the longer, flabby expression sounds more formal. Unfortunately, these flabby expressions are not brief, and they may even reduce a sentence's clarity. Be on the lookout for flabby expressions. Table 4.7 provides you with examples of flabby expressions and how they can be fixed.

Table 4.7 Flabby expressions and their concise counterparts

Flabby expression	Concise expression
We are of the opinion that	We think
Please feel free to	Please
Despite the fact that	Although
Due to the fact that	Because
At your earliest convenience	Soon
In respect of the matter	Regarding

Avoid Long Lead-Ins

Long lead-ins are words that appear at the beginning of a sentence that don't add anything to the meaning of the sentence. These expressions often state something that is obvious to the reader. Consider the following expression:

This e-mail is to inform you of today's schedule change.

"This e-mail is to inform you" represents a long lead-in. The reader is aware that the message is in e-mail format because he or she is reading the e-mail. In addition, the message is informing the reader about a change. Therefore, telling the reader that he or she is being informed is unnecessary. Consider the more concise expression as shown in the following:

Today's schedule has changed.

Here's another example of a long lead-in. Try to think about the sentence from the reader's perspective.

I am writing this letter to thank those of you who attended yesterday's meeting.

The reader knows it is a letter because he or she is reading it. The reader also knows you wrote the letter because you will have signed it. Therefore, the lead-in is unnecessary and inhibits brevity. Here is one way the sentence could be fixed.

Thank you for attending yesterday's meeting.

Eliminate Redundancies

A redundant expression contains at least one unnecessary word because it creates repetition. Some redundant expressions are used so frequently that they can be hard to identify. For example, the expression *absolutely essential* is redundant. Something can be either essential or nonessential. There are no degrees of essentiality. If something is essential, it is essential. Therefore, modifying essential with *absolutely* is redundant. Here's a list of other common redundant expressions. You can find a rather lengthy list at about.com.[8]

- Advance warning
- Filled to capacity
- Final outcome
- Rules and regulations
- Visible to the eye
- Repeat again

Conclusion

In this chapter, we hope to have provided you with simple tools for becoming a better business writer. You should have learned that good writers follow a process in how they prepare for the writing process, do research, and conduct proofreading and revising. We also provided you with some tools to help you achieve the ABCs of business writing: accuracy, brevity, and clarity.

Box 4.6 provides you with a summary of this chapter's takeaways. In Chapter 5, we turn our attention to advice for writing common finance documents.

Box 4.6 Chapter 4 takeaways

1. Begin the writing process by focusing on the three "P"s of message preparation: purpose, people, and placement.
2. Organize most of your writing using the CCSU Guide to Writing: Communicate the issue(s) or problem(s), clarify your approach to the issue(s) or problem(s), scrutinize your approach, and utilize your approach to resolve the issue(s) or solve the problem(s).
3. Be thorough in your approach to research.
4. Proofread and revise your writing using the four "F" words: format, filling, feeling, and filth.
5. Avoid common writing errors that work against your credibility and your document's accuracy, brevity, and clarity.

CHAPTER 5

Preparing Common Business Documents Used in Finance

In Chapter 4, we provided you with a disciplined approach to the writing process. That process can be applied to a broad range of documents. In this chapter, we offer guidance for writing common documents in the finance field. Using redacted documents from real-world communications, we provide you with tips for writing routine, positive, negative message, and persuasive messages.

Writing Routine and Positive Messages

Routine messages include those messages you will write that elicit a neutral response from your audience. In many ways, these messages are easy to construct because you won't have the added work of overcoming audience objections to your message. Routine messages usually do one of two things: (a) Convey information to your audience or (b) seek clarification from your audience. Typical routine messages include announcements about new or modified policies, information about upcoming meetings, routine reports (e.g., travel reports and sales reports), and denials of minor requests.

When writing routine messages, you should usually use the direct approach. In the opening of the message, identify the main idea of the message. Then, you provide a brief overview of the message's major points. For longer messages, you may want to set off each of the major points by using a bulleted list. In the body, provide all of the details needed by your audience. Finally, provide a brief, cordial closing. If the reader needs to take action, then make sure that you call the reader to action.

Consider the sample routine message in Box 5.1. The memo is an actual activity report submitted to a client by a consultant. Clients often

Box 5.1 Typical routine message

```
 1                          MEMORANDUM
 2
 3    TO:        Project Director, Ph.D.
 4    FROM:      Consultant, Ph.D.
 5    DATE:      February 01, 20XX
 6    RE:        Activity Report and Invoice for January 20XX
 7
 8    For your records, please accept this memorandum outlining work relative to project XXX-
 9    XXXX, review the attached invoice, and submit payment. In addition to an outline of the scope
10    of the work performed, this memo contains a list of the actual work performed in the last month.
11
12    For project XXX-XXXX, you retained my services to provide expertise in social-science
13    research methods, management science, and marketing communications. The project is designed
14    to advance the Center's research agenda and enhance the Center's performance on existing
15    and/or future grants, contracts, and/or projects. I have been retained to work on project XXX-
16    XXXX for the contract period of October 1, 20XX – Feb. 29, 20XX.
17
18    During the month of January, I worked on the following four major activities:
19
20        1. Analyzed primary data – I conducted multivariate analysis of the data collected from last
21           quarter's survey of residents in the target region. I submitted a report with preliminary
22           findings.
23        2. Conducted secondary research – In support of the data analysis and findings, I carried out
24           a literature search to provide a frame and context.
25        3. Outlined the final report – The final report is due at the end of February. In preparation
26           for writing the report, I spoke with the project manager, reviewed the information and
27           data we collected, and began developing an outline for the final report.
28        4. Began writing the final report – I started to prepare the first draft of the final report.
29
30    Thank you again for the opportunity to help the Center on this vital project. Please review the
31    attached invoice and submit payment within the next 30 days. If you have any questions or
32    concerns, please contact me.
33
34
35    Attachment: Invoice XXXXX-XXXXX-020120XX
```

request activity reports from their consultants each time the consultant submits an invoice for payment. As you can see, the memo follows our advice for writing routine messages. In particular, look at the following portions of the memo:

- Lines 8–9: The writer makes clear the memo's main idea.
- Lines 9–10: The writer provides an overview of the message's major points.
- Lines 12–28: The writer expands on the overview provided in the introduction.
- Lines 30–32: The writer closes cordially and calls the reader to action.

Positive messages are a pleasure to draft because you have the advantage of knowing your audience will be happy. Positive messages include announcing positive earnings and sales data, announcing employee promotions, saying yes to requests, and loan quotes. Similar to routine messages, you want to identify the main idea right away in the opening. Then, provide the reader with an overview of the major points that will be included in the message's body. In the body, provide the reader with all necessary information, including information about action the reader needs to take, if any. Write a cordial closing, referring back to the positive news, if that is appropriate.

In Box 5.2, you can see how our approach is put to use. The message is an actual e-mail message from a nonprofit organization to a student in Jason's class who participated in a letter-writing contest to help the nonprofit raise money. On Lines 3–4, the writer gets right to the point. On Lines 4–5, the writer provides an overview of the body. Lines 7–11 give the reader the information that needs to be submitted in order to cash in on the reward. The writer closes cordially and refers back to the positive news.

The letter in Box 5.3 is a positive news message. It is an actual loan quote letter that we've redacted in order to use in this book. As you can see, this letter follows our advice on delivering good news:

- Lines 13–14: The writer delivers the main idea.
- Lines 14–16: The writer provides an overview of the message's body.

Box 5.2 E-mail conveying positive news

1	Dear XXXXX:
2	
3	Congratulations on being selected as the winner of Team MAD's best persuasive
4	letter contest! You will need to provide us with some information to receive extra
5	course credit from your professor and special recognition at our annual banquet.
6	
7	To receive your extra credit and appropriate recognition, please provide us with
8	two pieces of information. Write us an email at XXXX@gmail.com and include your:
9	
10	• student ID number and
11	• class section number.
12	
13	Once we receive your email, we will contact you with details about the annual
14	banquet. Congratulations again for winning this contest. Your letter will help make a
15	difference in the lives of many people in Connecticut!
16	
17	Sincerely,
18	XXX XXXXX

Box 5.3 Loan quote

Finance Associates, Inc.

1   June 2, 2016
2
3   Mr. Joe Soandsew
4   Needscapital Corporation
5   33 Anywhere Rd
6   Anytown, CT 06000
7
8   RE: Britain Plaza, New Britain, CT (the "Property"), a 164,297 sf multi tenanted
9   shopping center anchored by a large national retailer.
10
11 Dear Mr. Soandsew,
12
13 Yankee Loan Company (Yankee or the "Lender") is pleased to provide you with this
14 term sheet for a Senior Loan for this Property through Lenders Direct. Please review
15 the terms. If they are acceptable, Lenders Direct will issue a formal application that
16 will provide more details.
17
18 Please note that this is not a commitment to lend but rather serves as an indication
19 of our interest in pursuing this transaction based on the following terms and
20 conditions.
21

Borrower	To-be formed bankruptcy-remote, single purpose entity ("SPE"). The General Partner or Managing Member shall also be a bankruptcy-remote SPE.
Purpose	Fund expenses relating to acquisition of the Property carry and provide up to $1,000,000 in additional funds subject to the achievement of certain income targets. Total project cost of $7,000,000 consisting of acquisition and related costs of $6,000,00 and renovation costs of $1,0000,00.
Borrower Equity	$2,200,000
Senior Loan Amount	$6,200,000 funded as follows: At closing $5,000,000, Upon achievement of a stabilized occupancy of 85% of rentable space and a debt service cover of 1.2X based on the trailing 6 months NOI: $1,200,000 will be available through our future funding option.
Rate	Fixed based on Ten Year US Treasury + 135 bps for the initial funding. Pricing for the future funding IS subject to market conditions.
LTV	85%
Amortization	I/O for three years, 30-year amortization for balance of term.
Prepayment	Locked out to prepayment for 36 months, payoff in whole thereafter based on Treasury Yield Maintenance. Prepayment at par during last

	three months of loan term.
Fee	1% on total loan of $6,200,000
Term	10 years
Guaranty	The Borrowing entity and its principals ("Guarantors") will execute (A) a hazardous substances indemnity agreement with respect to the Property, (B) a guaranty covering those certain standard "carve-outs" to the non-recourse provision set forth in the Loan documents. Guarantor to have and maintain a net worth of at least $10 million exclusive of the equity in the Property.
Security	First priority perfected first mortgage or deed of trust covering the Property, first priority security interest in Borrower owned furniture, fixtures
Collateral	The Property is certain real property known as Britain Plaza, New Britain, CT.
Term Sheet Expiration	Friday, June 10, 2016

22
23 Please review this term sheet and contact me by Friday, June 10, 2016 to let us
24 know whether you accept the terms. This letter should not be construed as a
25 commitment to make the proposed Loan. If you accept the terms, Lender's
26 determination to proceed with the proposed transaction shall be subject to, among
27 other things, its due diligence and approval of its credit committee.
28
29 Yours truly,
30
31 Yankee Loan Company
32 By: Finance Associates, Inc., its advisor
33
34 {signature}
35 John Jones
36 Senior Vice President

- Lines 18–20 and the table: The writer provides the loan quote needed for the reader to make a decision about acceptance of the terms.
- Lines 23–27: The writer calls the reader to action and describes what to expect in the future.
- Line 29: The writer closes cordially.

Writing Negative Messages

In the finance profession, you will undoubtedly have to write negative messages. You may have to deny credit to a client, report on losses, or tell job candidates that they did not get the job, among other things. Regardless of the purpose for delivering negative messages, you will want to keep the following goals in mind:

- Deliver the negative messages
- Make sure that your reader accepts the conclusion
- Demonstrate that you are fair
- Limit your liability
- Avoid inviting a back-and-forth about the news
- Minimize the damage to your reader

It is important in delivering the negative messages that you avoid being bad. Your reader's feelings matter. You need to tell the truth and deliver the negative messages, but it is critical that you do your best to minimize the negative impact of the message. You may be saying no to your reader today, but who knows what the future may hold for your relationship. The approach you take in constructing your message will help you achieve your goals when delivering negative messages.

When writing negative messages, you should usually use an indirect approach, for all of the reasons we discussed in Chapter 4. Consider opening your message with a buffer. A buffer is a neutral statement that gently prepares the reader for the negative messages to come. Readers expect to see words such as "congratulations" when the news is good. So, a gentle neutral statement often tells readers that the news is going to be bad before they actually see the news. You also want to keep the focus of attention off your reader. You can accomplish this by explaining the decision-making process that led to your conclusion. When you close, try to make what Jason calls "a future-looking statement." In other words, try to say something positive about the future. You may be saying no today, but the reader has a positive future to look forward to.

You have already read the positive message that one of Jason's students received from a nonprofit organization for winning a letter-writing contest. The other finalists received a negative message informing them that they did not win the contest. The negative message is in Box 5.4. As we highlight how this message follows our advice, you should also consider the differences between this message and the positive message that was sent to the winner.

As you can see in Lines 3–4, the letter opens with a neutral buffer before delivering the negative messages in Lines 4–5. The writer demonstrates fairness in the body of the message by describing the decision-making process in Lines 7–12. Finally, the writer closes by thanking the reader and making a future-looking statement.

You can also see how our advocated approach to negative messages can be applied to common finance documents. Consider the budget memo in Box 5.5 to residents of a housing complex from their board of directors. Line 8 opens with a positive buffer. The negative messages is delivered on Lines 9–10. You can see on Lines 11–15 how the Board describes the process they went through over the year to keep fees low. In the last two lines, the Board talks about the future and says that the fee increase is "a practice that will enhance the value of your unit."

Box 5.4 Sample negative message

1	Dear XXXXX:
2	
3	Thanks for writing a persuasive letter for Team MAD's best persuasive letter
4	contest. Your letter was given serious consideration, but we have selected another
5	letter as this year's winner.
6	
7	Let me explain our selection process for you. First, your name and any other
8	identifying information were removed to ensure confidentiality. Then, a panel of
9	judges read all of the letters. Next, they used a scoring rubric to rate each letter on
10	five dimensions of quality. The letters were then ranked based on the total number
11	of points received You received the third highest number of points. Finally, the
12	judges contacted all finalists.
13	
14	We are grateful for the time and energy that you committed to this amazing cause.
15	Please consider joining our team to help us make a difference.
16	
17	Cordially,
18	XXX XXXXX

Box 5.5 Negative messages budget memo

1	JADEN PARK
2	C/O THE BOARD OF DIRECTORS
3	PO BOX 555, JADEN PARK, CT 06000
4	
5	
6	

To: The Residents of Jaden Park

From: The Board of Directors

Date: May 18, 2016

Subject: 2016 – 2017 Budget

---

7   Dear Homeowners,

8   Thank you for entrusting the Board with the work of ensuring the value of our units. You will
9   shortly receive your 2016-2017 coupon book. The maintenance fee will increase to $371.00, a
10   6.89% increase over the amount you have been paying for the last two (2) years.

11   Let me describe how the Board arrived at this decision. As you are aware and as the attached data
12   demonstrate, costs have gone up over the last two (2) years. The Board has worked hard to avoid
13   fee increases. In certain cases, the Board has been able to lower certain expenses. In other cases,
14   expenses have gone up. In some other cases, expenses could not be contracted on a fixed-fee basis.
15   After much discussion, the Board concluded that fee increases were necessary.

16   The Board believes that we must all adequately plan for the future. To that end, we are
17   endeavoring to set aside the correct reserves, a practice that will enhance the value of your unit.

Writing Persuasive Messages

In writing persuasive messages, your decision to use a direct or indirect approach will ultimately depend on your reader's reaction to your request. The more inclined your reader is to say no, the more likely you are to move away from a direct approach toward an indirect approach. In being persuasive, you need to consider a few things.

First, always answer the What's In It For Me? (WIIFM) question. If you want your readers to say yes to a request or carry out a certain action, they have to know what's in it for them. Tell them what's to gain or lose. Second, discuss the benefits of your ideas, not the features. Jason tells his students that one of the best ways to learn about persuasive communication is to watch QVC television. In particular, watch Mr. David Venable, host of *In the Kitchen with David*. When he sells food products or kitchen accessories, he doesn't focus on what the accessories are made from or what the cooking process is like. He tastes the food or uses the accessory. If the experience is particularly delightful, Mr. Venable does the happy dance. It may sound silly, but he is selling the benefit of the products, and he sells millions of units. Third, consider the factors driving your reader toward saying yes and those factors restraining your reader from saying yes.

Enhance Your Credibility and Likeability

Volumes of research exist on how we can make our messages more persuasive, and one could probably organize a small army with the gurus who offer advice in this area. We will add our names to that list by sharing some simple things to keep in mind when crafting persuasive messages.

Earlier in this book, we discussed that credibility fuels your communication. Nowhere is that more true than in crafting persuasive messages. One of the things we have learned from research is that people commit what is called the genetic fallacy. In other words, people have trouble separating the message from the sender. They are more likely to accept a bad idea from a genius than they are a brilliant idea from a ne'er-do-well. The two characteristics that seem to matter most when these people assess senders of persuasive appeals are credibility and likeability.[1]

Credibility comprises your trustworthiness and competence. So, the recipients of your persuasive messages will ask themselves, "Can I trust this person, and can I think this person knows what he or she is talking about?" Look at your professional network. Do you surround yourself with people who can't be trusted and don't know what they're talking about? We certainly hope not. And this is important because we all tend to naturally like people to whom we ascribe greater credibility. In many cases, you will find that if you are perceived as credible and likeable, a good bit of your persuasive work has already been done.

But what if your reader doesn't know who you are? Are there things you can do in your written messages that will enhance your credibility and likeability? Yes, you can enhance your credibility and likeability in the following ways:

- If you have expertise, share it. Don't assume people know your background.
- Show your reader that you've done your research.
- Describe how you have delivered on your promises in the past.
- Demonstrate that you understand your reader's perspective.
- Demonstrate a genuine concern for your reader's well-being.
- Share personal stories—when they are appropriate—to show your audience you trust them enough to share their confidence.

- Establish common ground with your readers. Highlight
  shared goals.

As you write those persuasive appeals, remember that your message needs to speak about both your ideas and you. Your audience is assessing both.

Consider the e-mail, which is a real-world persuasive message, Box 5.6. In the e-mail, the writer is trying to sell a product to improve lease administration productivity within the reader's corporate real estate firm. The writer does a number of things well. First, the message attempts to answer the WIIFM question. In fact, on Lines 12–19, the message suggests that the new product will help the reader find answers to many important questions. The writer also establishes credibility by making a

Box 5.6 *Sample persuasive message*

1	From:	Jaden Aaron
2	Sent:	Wednesday, June 1, 2016
3	To:	edwinhenry@mailme.com
4	Subject:	Edwin – Can we help you get more out of your lease administration activities?
5		
6	Hello Edwin:	
7		
8	Improving internal productivity can be the fastest route to improved bottom line
9	performance. To get the pulse on your department, we have created a scorecard review that
10	leverages our depth of experience and produces a heat map that clearly identifies and
11	begins to quantify opportunities for productivity improvement. It provides an excellent tool
12	for evaluating how much you have to gain by making internal changes. Let us help you
13	discover:
14	
15	1. Where do productivity opportunities exist within my department?
16	2. What would it take to make changes? How do we get started?
17	3. Do our operational activities support our business strategy?
18	4. Does our department return enough to the business?
19	5. Am I getting the greatest benefit out of today's best practices?
20	
21	These are tough questions for every executive to ask, especially for corporate real estate
22	executives like you. Helping you integrate a disciplined performance management strategy
23	into your lease administration activities is what we specialize in. Aaron Administration has
24	more than twenty years of in-depth experience helping corporate and retail real estate
25	departments save money and become more productive. Recent projects include helping a
26	large cinema company refine its processes, better utilize its technology, and right-size its
27	staffing levels. Another recent project recovered more than $1,000,000 in over-payments
28	and billing errors.
29	
30	I invite your inquiries and welcome the opportunity to explore this further with you. Please
31	let me know your availability for a short intro call.
32	
33	Best regards,
34	
35	Jaden Aaron
36	Senior Vice President
37	Aaron Administration, LLC

reference to the company's areas of expertise and its track record of success (Lines 21–28). The e-mail closes with a clear call to action.

Understand the Six Principles of Influence

In addition to understanding how your audience responds to you, you should also understand how they respond to important social cues. To help you better understand these cues, we encourage you to read the work of Dr. Robert Cialdini on the six principles of influence (see Box 5.7).[2] We share the six principles here with ideas for how you can apply them to your persuasive messages, but to master the principles, you should read his books.

We have already discussed the liking principle. When people like you, they are more likely to say yes to a request you make of them. For example, LuLaRoe parties are becoming increasingly common (think Tupperware or Pampered Chef parties, but with dresses). Your friend hosts a LuLaRoe party and invites you over to try on some dresses. When she asks you to buy a dress, you are more likely to say yes simply because you like your friend. We often choose friends who are similar to us. Therefore, one of the best ways to make yourself more likeable is to demonstrate how you are similar to your audience.

The principle of authority teaches us that people are more likely to comply with requests when they come from perceived authority figures. The term "authority" sounds a little heavy-handed, so you can think of it as credibility. As we suggested previously, you have a number of tactics at your disposal to enhance your credibility in your written messages. Employ those tactics.

Box 5.7 Robert Cialdini's six principles of persuasion

1. Liking
2. Authority
3. Consistency and commitment
4. Reciprocity
5. Scarcity
6. Social proof

The principle of reciprocity teaches us that people are more likely to comply with your requests when they owe you a favor. One of the best ways to make yourself more persuasive is to make yourself helpful. Get into the habit of doing good for others. Your favors are not only a great way to build relationships, but they are also a great way to getting to yes before you even make a request.

The principle of commitment and consistency teaches us that when people commit to goals, they are more likely to work toward those goals. People also want to be seen as acting consistently with their expressed values and ideas. We both love doing CrossFit, and at both of our boxes (i.e., gyms), members are encouraged to write their fitness goals on a whiteboard for everyone to see. It's a great motivational tool because it holds the members publicly accountable for their own goals. One way you can use this principle in your writing is to remind your readers about their goals and values. Then, you can demonstrate how your request is in line with those goals and values.

The scarcity principle teaches us that people want more those things they can't have. Diamonds are expensive because their flow to the marketplace is tightly restricted. We see the scarcity principle in action when products are in short supply, when offers are for a limited time, and when few seats are available. Scarcity creates a sense of urgency for your reader. Put timelines on your proposals, demonstrate how rare an opportunity you are presenting, encourage your readers to act, and remind them of what they stand to lose if they don't comply with your requests.

The social proof principle teaches us that when people are unsure of what they should do, they look to see what others are doing. When making persuasive appeals, you can demonstrate for your readers that other people who are just like your readers are complying with your request. Social proof is a powerful tool of influence.

Conclusion

In this chapter, we offered guidance for writing common documents in the finance field. Using real-world documents, we provided you with tips for how to write routine, positive, negative, and persuasive messages (see Table 5.1 for key takeaways). We also highlighted Robert Cialdini's six principles of influence to help you understand simple ways to gain compliance for your requests. In the next chapter, we turn our focus away from writing business messages to preparing and delivering effective business presentations.

Table 5.1 Chapter 5 takeaways

Message type	Common examples	Tips
Positive	Positive earnings Positive sales data Employee promotions Approving requests Loan quotes	• Use a direct approach. • Provide an overview of the major points. • Provide all necessary information, including information about action the reader needs to take. • Write a cordial closing, referring back to the positive news, if that is appropriate.
Bad news	Denial of financing Loan rejection Poor investment Performance Dividend reduction Increase in costs or fees	• Use an indirect approach. • Use a buffer. • Keep the focus off of your reader. • Demonstrate your fairness by describing decision-making process. • Use a forward-looking statement to close.
Persuasive	Sales proposal Project proposal Financing requests Appeals Loan application Product marketing	• Answer the WIIFM question. • Discuss benefits, not features. • Consider driving and restraining forces. • Enhance your credibility and likeability. • Use the six principles of persuasion.

CHAPTER 6

Preparing and Delivering Finance Presentations with Maximum Impact

Presentations are a reality for finance professionals. No product or service offered by your company hit the marketplace until a series of presentations were delivered. Whether you enjoy delivering presentations or hide behind your computer screen in hopes that nobody will EVER ask you to deliver a presentation, you might as well face the fact that you will have to deliver presentations throughout your career.

Now that you've given that fact a minute to settle in, let's get to work enhancing your presentation skills. In this chapter, we help you make appropriate choices at each stage of the presentation design and delivery processes. You will learn how to:

1. Craft a powerful introduction, body, and conclusion
2. Organize content for best results
3. Develop an effective call to action
4. Deliver with confidence
5. Build multimedia slides that won't bore your audience members and insult their intelligence

By following our advice, you will transform into a virtuous presenter. So, let's begin the journey by exploring the four virtues of business presentations.

Becoming a Virtuous Presenter

You may read the phrase "virtuous presenter" and wonder if maybe we're setting unreasonably high expectations. We have a friend who works in

Box 6.1 *The four virtues of the virtuous presenter*

Fortitude—having the courage necessary to get in front of an audience and be the presentation

Prudence—demonstrating the wisdom to make the right choices and put in the hard work necessary to design and deliver a powerful presentation

Justice—treating your audience fairly by not putting them through a boring presentation with all the problems that you don't like to experience when you're an audience member

Temperance—exercising control over your use of multimedia software and showing restraint over your tendency to rely on defaults

---

consulting who likes to use the phrase "aim for perfection to achieve excellence." We agree. Given the significance of business presentations, modern professionals should not aim to be good presenters; they should try to be the best. They should try to be virtuous.

A virtue is nothing more than a quality that is good, useful, or desirable. People can be virtuous in a number of ways. We focus our discussion on four virtues that some of you may have heard before (see Box 6.1):

1. Fortitude
2. Prudence
3. Justice
4. Temperance

These are the four cardinal virtues in the Catholic faith. Although we don't digress into a discussion on religion, we do argue that virtuous presenters exhibit these four virtues. As you will see, the four virtues are not mutually exclusive. For now, let's examine them one at a time.

Fortitude

The first virtue of the virtuous presenter is fortitude. We define presentation fortitude as having the courage necessary to get in front of an audience and be the presentation. People fear delivering presentations. In fact, you've probably heard that when asked about their greatest fears, people often rank fear of public speaking higher than death. Comedian Jerry Seinfeld used to quip that people at a funeral would rather be in the casket than delivering the eulogy.

Why are people so afraid of public speaking? Some social psychologists argue that the answer lies in human evolution. Humans are social beings, in part, because we once lived in a world where we were not at the apex of the food pyramid. On a bad day, our ancestors could easily find themselves on the dinner menu of larger predators. Being social provided humans with the ability to alert one another about danger and to work together to defend against attack. Finding oneself ostracized from the group could spell doom. In a recent *Psychology Today* article, Dr. Glenn Croston related these primitive fears to our modern fear of public speaking:[1]

> When faced with standing up in front of a group, we break into a sweat because we are afraid of rejection. And at a primal level, the fear is so great because we are not merely afraid of being embarrassed, or judged. We are afraid of being rejected from the social group, ostracized and left to defend ourselves all on our own. We fear ostracism still so much today it seems, fearing it more than death, because not so long ago getting kicked out of the group probably really was a death sentence.

Our fears of delivering presentations can often lead to poor practices. Fear can cause us to avoid situations where we may be called upon to speak. But avoiding those situations in business can have deleterious effects on your career trajectory. Those with fortitude seize those opportunities. Jennifer Savini, a senior internal auditor and senior financial analyst for a major provider of health insurance, told us about the role of communication and presentation skills in her career.

> Good communication skills are needed in order to meet expectations in regards to my job requirements; however, excellent communications skills are required in order to exceed expectations for my role. ... I had the opportunity to prepare and execute a pre-

sentation for executive level presidents in my firm. ... There were other members of my team that possessed greater knowledge but lacked the communication skills necessary to present. This allowed me to gain valuable exposure to important decision makers.[2]

Jennifer Savini
Sr. Internal Auditor/
Sr. Financial Analyst
Health Insurance Provider

Our fears may lead us to do what we perceive as safe. In other words, we look at what other presenters do and mimic their presentation behaviors. That works well if you're observing people who are excellent presenters. If not, then you're just copying their mistakes. And that is too frequently the case. For example, you should NEVER begin your speech with "Hello, my name is ...." In most business presentation situations, the audience already knows your name. And if they don't know it, will it hurt them to wait 20 seconds to hear it? Audiences MUST be engaged in the first few seconds of a presentation. Simply telling them your name will not engage them. We see other people start presentations that way all the time, so we copy that "safe" behavior.

Fear also causes us to do things like read from prepared statements or from our multimedia slides. That is insulting to our audience members.

But the alternative is to actually be the presentation—to be the center of attention. That is scary!

Virtuous presenters have some fear, but they have even more fortitude. They think about what they're afraid will go wrong during a presentation, and they take the steps to prepare for those possible scenarios. They seize the opportunities presented to them. They practice until they know their material. They practice the right way. They don't hide from their audience. They engage their audience. They become the presentation by preparing effective slides and using best practices instead of doing what they think is safe. If you think you're up for the challenge, we give you tips to put your fortitude to work for you! Besides, we can *almost* guarantee that a predator won't eat you during a presentation.

Prudence

Presenters who demonstrate prudence exercise the wisdom to make the right choices and put in the hard work necessary to design and deliver a powerful presentation. Too many people deliver lackluster presentations simply because they did not make the right choices about their time management and failed to prepare themselves adequately.

Virtuous presenters conduct their audience and situation analysis. They understand their audience before delivering their presentations. They think in advance about the major points they will make and the data they will need to make those points. They consider how to organize those points. They think about the type of persuasive appeal they will make. They design slides that complement their presentation and avoid common errors like creating slides with too much text. They consider whether they need handouts. They put in the time to practice.

Justice

Justice is like the golden rule of presentations. You demonstrate justice when you treat your audience fairly by not putting them through a boring presentation with all the problems that you don't like to experience when you're an audience member. We have had the displeasure of sitting through hundreds, maybe thousands, of boring presentations. And we're sure you have seen some presentations that made you roll your eyes and wish you were anywhere else in the world.

These boring presentations share some key characteristics, all of which are under the speakers' control. In these presentations, the speaker:

- Does not know the material
- Did not know the audience
- Did not practice
- Read from prepared notes or off the multimedia slides
- Prepared slides filled with words
- Failed to engage the audience through eye contact, vocal dynamics, or body language
- Went over the allotted time

We're sure that you agree that these presentations are atrocious. You can identify the characteristics that make a presentation boring. In fact, most people know a bad presentation when they see one. You don't need to be a trained expert. And yet, people continue to make the same mistakes. That's not fair! Presenters who deliver presentations with these characteristics have no sense of justice. They are torturing their audiences. Let's resolve to do better. Let's be virtuous. Let's take the steps necessary to demonstrate that we have a sense of justice and we respect our audiences.

Temperance

You can demonstrate temperance by exercising control over your use of multimedia software and showing restraint over your tendency to rely on defaults. We once heard a comedian say that the reason why bullet points are called bullet points is because of the bullets that audience members want to put in presenters who overuse bullet points (see Figure 6.1).

Perhaps you've heard of "death by PowerPoint." This is the idea that business audiences have seen too many PowerPoint slides.

So let's do away with PowerPoint and related multimedia slide software! Not so fast. The software is not the problem. The problem is our

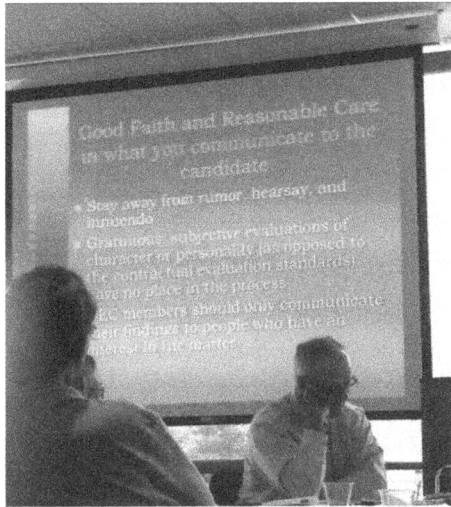

Figure 6.1 Audience member experiencing death by PowerPoint

use of the software. We tell our students that engineers and IT people created PowerPoint. They are not presentation experts. So why take slide design suggestions from them? Exercise your own discretion and your own imagination in constructing slides. Why use default slide layouts, default fonts, or default anything? When we rely on defaults, we bore our audiences to "death." And we certainly don't create anything that's memorable. Later in this chapter, we give you detailed advice for slide design. For now, consider the following guidelines when thinking about your use of multimedia slide software.

- Use multimedia slide software only when necessary.
- Use your imagination. Do not rely on defaults.
- Use visuals that evoke an emotional response. Do not simply fill the slides with words and bullet points.
- Display only that information or data that is necessary to make your point.
- Avoid reading from your slides.

If you allow these simple guidelines to direct your use of multimedia slide software, you will decrease the likelihood of putting your audience through "death by PowerPoint." And you'll be one step closer to being a virtuous presenter.

Now that you have a better understanding of what it takes to be a virtuous presenter, let's take a look at the major elements of a business presentation. In the following sections, we take you through the process of preparing a business presentation. First, we ask you to answer the following question about your presentations: *What's the big idea?*

Developing the "Big Idea"

Presentation professional Nancy Duarte writes about developing a presentation's big idea in at least two of her recent books.[3] She argues that you should see your presentation as world changing. If most of your business presentations are persuasive in nature, then aren't you in fact changing the world in some way? If you spend some time thinking about that idea, you will discover it's quite powerful. Putting yourself into the frame of mind created by the thought that you're changing the world will have a number of meaningful outcomes for your presentation preparation and delivery. And one of the first places where we see the impact of the "world-changing" attitude is in how you frame your presentation.

Most presenters, when asked about their presentation, will share with you their topic. For example, a speaker may tell you that he or she is preparing a "Summary of Company X's financial ratios," or building a presentation about "an investment opportunity." Those are topics and they sound emotionally detached and not terribly compelling. In fact, those topics wouldn't require a presentation. The speaker could instead write up a review and e-mail it to the decision makers.

Think about why one might conduct a summary of financial ratios. One reason for doing so is to make recommendations about buying, selling, or staying away from an investment in a company's common stock. So what's the big idea?

According to Nancy Duarte, a big idea requires two elements to be impactful. First, the big idea needs to share your perspective and tell the audience what they should do. If you are making a persuasive appeal, it's important to be very clear from the beginning what you need from your audience. Second, the big idea should tell the audience what is at stake.

What will happen if the audience takes your advice or fails to take your advice? State your big idea as a complete sentence and let it guide you through all the decisions you will make when preparing the presentation. Instead of saying your presentation is "a summary of Company X's financial ratios," you could say something like "You should not purchase common stock in Company X because its financial ratios indicate it will likely be bankrupt within the next six months, and you will lose your investment."

Not only is the big idea as expressed previously more powerful, but it will also affect the way you present the information. Instead of thinking about simply presenting data on things like an Altman's Z-score, the big idea will make you think about how you can best make your case. What information is required to be more persuasive? How should the information be organized to have a maximum impact? What types of persuasive appeals should you make? Should you develop handouts or multimedia slides? How much involvement do you want from your audience?

These decisions are all influenced by how you think about what your presentation is about and what you know about your audience and situation. Now that you have a sense for writing a big idea, let's take a look at the basic parts of a presentation, beginning with the beginning.

Starting with a Bang

If you recall from the beginning of this chapter, we suggested that one should never start a presentation with "Hello, my name is ...." It isn't virtuous. Many presenters begin their presentation that way because it is safe and provides a soft opening to the presentation's content. In most business presentation situations, the audience will know who you are because they work with you, you've been introduced, or your name is on a handout or on the multimedia slide at which they're looking. Even if your audience doesn't know your name, does it really matter if they have to wait an extra moment or two to hear it?

The introduction is your opportunity to hook your audience, to direct their attention to your big idea. Introductions are brief, relative to the body of the presentation, but they are important and have a lot to do. In your introductions, you will need to:

- Capture the audience's attention
- Explain your big idea
- Identify yourself (if you haven't been introduced)
- Establish your credibility
- Provide a road map for the presentation

At the beginning of any presentation, the first thing you need to do is capture the audience's attention. Even at meetings where your presentation is the main purpose of the meeting, your audience members will all be thinking of different things when you begin. You need to get them all on the same page and give them a compelling reason to listen to the presentation. We do describe some ways that you can hook your audience, but keep in mind what the hook will do. The hook puts the audience in a particular frame of mind. It sets the mood. What frame of mind or emotion do you want to evoke during the presentation? The hook creates a theme for the presentation. You should refer to the hook throughout the presentation. The repetition can make your big idea and supporting points easier to remember. Let's take a look at tactics you can use to capture your audience's attention (see Box 6.2).

Box 6.2 Tactics for capturing audience attention

Share a compelling or novel statistic

Tell an emotional story

Describe a serious problem

Answer the WIIFM question

Ask a rhetorical question

Use humor

Show a captivating video

- Share a compelling or novel statistic. Note that we didn't simply say *share a statistic*. The statistic has to be something that startles your audience and makes them think. That means the statistic has to be truly compelling for your audience.

- Tell an emotional story. People enjoy stories and they are an excellent means for humanizing your topic. Provide your audience with a story that exemplifies the stakes related to your big idea. In some cases, you can even provide your audience with a realistic hypothetical example. You can use stories to create a cliffhanger for your audience. Cliffhangers make it easier to refer back to the introduction and people will pay attention because they want to know how stories end. Stories should involve conflict that gets resolved. Ideally, you can empower your audience through your presentation to resolve the conflict.

- Describe a serious problem. If you are attempting to make a persuasive appeal, you can always paint a picture of the world as it exists today versus the world as it could be if the audience follows your advice. Contrast is a great way to help audience members think about your big idea.

- Answer the What's In It For Me? (WIIFM) question. One of the easiest ways to get the audience to focus on your topic is to tell them upfront what is in it for them.

- Ask a rhetorical question. These questions are designed to get audience members thinking. For instance, if you believe that buying a company's common stock will lead to huge losses for your audience, you could begin the presentation by saying, "If our company loses $10 million because of a poor investment choice, how many people would lose their jobs in order for us to make up for that loss?"

- Use humor. As long as the situation is appropriate, you can tell a joke. The joke should be tasteful and never made at the audience's expense.

- Show a captivating video. Be sure the video is relevant and brief. Remember that you are the presentation and you won't want a video to do the talking for you. If you use a video, try to test out the equipment in advance, if possible.

Be creative with your attention-grabbing hook. You can use some of these tactics in combination. All of these tactics take more time than merely introducing yourself, but they all provide a much higher return on your investment of time and energy.

After you captured the audience's attention, share with them your big idea. You'll share with them a bold position along with a picture of what's at stake. The audience will then need a reason to trust you. So, you'll need to follow up the big idea with statements that establish your credibility. Here is where you'll need to show your audience that you have direct experience with the matter at hand or have done extensive homework. Tell your audience what makes you a person whose big idea should be considered seriously.

Finally, you should provide your audience with a road map. What are the three to five points that you will discuss in the body of the presentation that will offer support for your big idea? You may have many points that support the big idea, but your audience will be able to remember only so many of them. So make strategic decisions about which points are most important and limit the presentation body to those three to five points.

To help you make that decision, ask yourself, "What are the three to five things my audience must remember in order for this presentation to be successful?" You will want to repeat these points at least three times throughout the presentation; once in the introduction, once in the body, and once in the conclusion (see Figure 6.2).

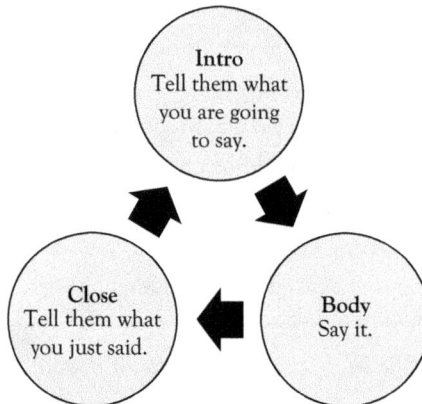

Figure 6.2 Repetition of supporting points in presentations

The presentation itself is like a repeating cycle, where repetition reinforces the points you want the audience to remember. Here's an expression we share with our students and clients: "Tell them what you're going to say. Say it. Then, tell them what you just said."

Keeping Your Audience Engaged Through the Body

As we've just discussed, the body of your presentation will include three to five supporting points. In thinking about those points, you will want to sequence them for maximum impact. As a general rule, we tell people to put the most important point either first or last, because the audience will be more likely to remember them. Another way to organize your points for maximum impact is to create contrast, such as us versus them, best versus worst case scenario, the past (or present) versus the future, what can go wrong versus what can go right, and risk versus conservatism.

The supporting points will need to be buffered by sufficient evidence that you gathered while researching the topic. However, the body of the presentation is not simply the provision of supporting points and accompanying evidence. You still have to work hard to keep your audience engaged and awake. You have a number of options for doing so, including:

- Balancing emotion and logic
- Using effective imagery
- Using your delivery style

As we discussed in Chapter 2, it's important to consider the role of emotion in business communication. Business presentations should include logical arguments—features of products, primary and secondary evidence, and case studies. However, logical arguments are not always going to provoke the emotions required to be persuasive. So, balance product features with product benefits, primary and secondary evidence with suspenseful stories, and case studies with answers to the WIIFM question.

You can also use imagery to paint a more colorful picture of your data. The tools of imagery we can use include analogies, metaphors, similes, personal anecdotes or statistics, and best or worst case scenarios. If we take a presentation in which the speaker is trying to convince managers to rein in spending, the speaker may use the following devices to enhance imagery:

- Analogy—Solving our company's spending problems will require an intervention similar to helping a drug addict overcome an addiction. Our managers need tough love.
- Metaphor—Our company's spending problems are like a noose around the neck.
- Simile—Our manager's spending problem is creating a bubble in our budget that threatens to burst.
- Personal anecdote—My parents taught me to spend no more money than I actually have. Unfortunately, our managers did not have my parents raising them.
- Best or worst case scenario—If we can't put limits on our managers' spending, we will have to shut down facilities and lay off employees.

In addition to imagery, you can use your presentation delivery to keep audience members engaged. For now, we share some tips from the Presentation Zen Garr Reynolds. To keep your audience engaged, you should be engaged. Why should the audience care, if they don't believe you care? If your delivery style is too formal and devoid of emotion, then your audience will not feel emotionally engaged.

Remember that emotions are contagious; smiling and displaying natural, authentic emotions will help your audience's response to the presentation. You can stimulate your audience's curiosity by asking questions like "What do you think happens next?" and expressing your own curiosity by saying things like "How incredible!"[4] We return to delivery style in greater detail later in the chapter. For now, suffice it to say that you should move, make eye contact, modify your speaking voice to create emphasis, and speak loudly and clearly.

Closing Powerfully

A few years ago, Jason attended a national union event. At one of the presentations, the speaker made a powerful argument against the reduction of state economic support for higher education. The speaker was smart, witty, and well reasoned. He made clear points supported by data and personal anecdotes. It was an ideal presentation and quite moving. The speaker wanted the audience members to contact their state legislators to speak out against budget cuts for higher education. Jason never called his legislator. Why not?

Jason didn't call his legislator for the same reason that we are willing to bet most of the people in that room didn't make the call. The presentation's close was not well thought out. After spending the presentation about the negative consequences of budget cuts and the need for intervention, he merely said, "Thank you. Are there any questions?" The speaker must have invested considerable resources in putting that presentation together and it all fell apart at the end because he did not carefully consider the close. So now that we have an idea what an ineffective close looks like, let's consider what needs to go into a close and avoid wasting our efforts with a poor close. A conclusion needs to do the following things:

- Signal the impending close.
- Reiterate your big idea and supporting points.
- Make a specific call to action.
- Close memorably.

First, it must provide a signal to the audience that the presentation is about to end. Although it's a simple tactic, many speakers say, "Let me close by saying...." That little expression provides a signal to the audience that the presentation is coming to an end. Audience members tend to perk up when they believe the presentation is about to close, because it means they can leave and that they also have an obligation to acknowledge the conclusion (usually through applause). Abrupt closes, such as the one made by the union presenter did not take advantage of the opportunity to recapture the attention of any audience members who may have been daydreaming.

Once you signal the close of your presentation, you should reiterate your big idea and the supporting points. If they missed any of the points during the body of the presentation, the close presents one more opportunity to make the point. If they were paying attention, the repetition will help them retain the information.

After you've reminded your audience of the big idea and supporting points, challenge the audience with a specific call to action. Have you ever heard the expression *If you don't ask, you don't get*? It is equally true in presentations as it is in everyday life. This is your chance to tell the audience what you want them to do. You need to make it easy for your audience to comply. Empower your audience! The more barriers your audience members must overcome, the less likely they are to comply with your call to action. Empower your audience members to take the first steps to fulfilling your request as soon as possible. Convince your audience that if they take the appropriate actions, they will solve major problems, resolve conflict, overcome negative forces acting against them, make the future better than the present, or save the world!

In the case of our union presenter, he made no effort to overcome barriers. The presentation was delivered in Chicago to members from across the country. The speaker did not specifically ask the audience members to call their legislators. Even if he had made a call to action, what barriers were his audience members facing? They may not have known who their legislators were or how to find them. Even if they knew their legislators, they probably didn't know how to contact them. Once they contacted their legislators, what should they say?

Jason didn't make that phone call. He attended the conference for several more days before returning to Connecticut. In that time, other priorities crept into his life. He couldn't remember the details of the presentation. He didn't know what he was supposed to say. Faced with other demands for his time, he simply didn't do it. And we're willing to bet that the vast majority of people in that room also didn't call their legislators. Consider how differently that could have worked out had the presenter considered more carefully the close of his presentation.

Following your call to action, have a strong closing line. Avoid simply saying, "Thank you." It's safe and easy. We don't like safe and easy. The closing line should remind your audience about the introduction. If you told a cliffhanger in the introduction, then the close is your chance to finish the story. If your story involved conflict, then the close is where you resolve that conflict. If the presentation created contrast by discussing the past versus the future, here is your chance to paint a complete, beautiful picture of the future that lies ahead in contrast to the past that you painted in your introduction.

Delivering Like a Professional

Preparing an effective presentation and delivering an effective presentation are two distinctly different things. Some people are naturally gifted speakers. They are able to speak calmly and with confidence regardless of the situation. That said, presentation delivery skills are just that, skills that can be improved through practice. So, regardless of your comfort level, your skills can improve. Here are our best tips for delivering like a professional (see Box 6.3).

Be Authentic. Be Vulnerable

Have you ever started preparing yourself for a presentation with the hope that the presentation would be perfect? Delivering the perfect presentation is a noble goal. It's also the source of tremendous mental distress. Too many times we have seen perfectly good presenters fall apart because of the stress that the drive for perfection caused them.

Box 6.3 Tips for delivering like a professional

Be authentic. Be vulnerable.

Have a conversation. Be extemporaneous.

Speak loudly, clearly, and with conviction.

Move.

Dress appropriately.

Practice the right way.

You are not perfect (neither are we). In fact, your lack of perfection is part of what makes you human. What does a perfect presentation look like? We wouldn't know because we've never seen a perfect presentation. The best presentations are those presentations in which people are authentic and vulnerable. These presenters create real connections with their audiences because they themselves are being real. Let us repeat—the best presentations are those in which the speaker makes an authentic connection with the audience. Being yourself—flaws and all—is the secret to effective delivery style.

One great example of the imperfect but vulnerable delivery style is the (in)famous Monkey Boy speech by Steve Ballmer. Mr. Ballmer was CEO of Microsoft from 2000 to 2014 and is the current owner of the Los Angeles Clippers basketball team. If you ever want to see a truly authentic—if not unnerving—delivery style, Google "Steve Ballmer Monkey Boy." He delivered the Monkey Boy speech while at Microsoft. It opens with him running and dancing around the stage screaming "Woo!" He then opened his presentation breathlessly with the words "I have four words for you! I love this company!" This is authentic Steve Ballmer. He has had similar displays of emotion in other presentations. He is comfortable with being emotional and vulnerable. At his final presentation before leaving Microsoft, he cried openly in front of the audience. Mr. Ballmer is an authentic and memorable speaker. His presentations are far from perfect, but they have impact!

Maybe running, dancing, screaming, and crying are not your thing. If not, then don't act that way during your presentations. Be your authentic self. Have the bravery to make yourself vulnerable. Dr. Brené Brown is a social work professor who has dedicated her life to studying vulnerability and courage. She argues that being truly authentic means making yourself vulnerable. She wrote that "vulnerability sounds like truth and feels like courage. Truth and courage aren't always comfortable, but they're never weakness."[5] In addition to having great advice on the topic of vulnerability, she has an authentic delivery style. She is quiet and calm with a dry wit; but because she is authentic, she is still every bit as engaging as Mr. Ballmer.

In an impressive TEDx presentation on vulnerability, Dr. Brown gave excellent advice that applies not only to our approach to interpersonal relationships but also to engaging our audiences.[6] She said that we all struggle with being authentic and making ourselves vulnerable to others. In our efforts to avoid vulnerability, she said that people try to perfect things. As she put it, "We take fat from our butts and put it in our cheeks." And the result is a loss of authenticity. We believe that people do the same things with their presentations. In an effort to avoid the vulnerability associated with being authentic and making real connections, we focus our energy in the wrong places and try to perfect elements of our presentation (e.g., multimedia slides and individual words) while failing to pay attention to the fundamental need to simply connect. Dr. Brown also argued that we protect ourselves from vulnerability by pretending that what we do has no effect on others. The truth is we can't make our presentations perfect, and what we do matters. Embracing the vulnerability of imperfection can be liberating. So, as Dr. Brown says, "Lean into the vulnerability." An audience that connects with you and cares about you is always willing to forgive and overlook minor flaws.

Have a Conversation. Be Extemporaneous

One way to demonstrate authenticity is through an extemporaneous speaking style. This is a speaking style that allows you to use notes sparingly. Your audience will be bored to tears if you read from your notes. For the vast majority of us, reading sounds like reading. That's boring. Reading from our notes also causes us to lose eye contact with our audience. It is difficult to have a conversation with a person with whom you are not making eye contact. Eye contact allows us to engage with our audience and see how they react to what we are saying. It gives us the opportunity to make changes (such as adding clarification if audience members look confused) during a presentation.

Your notes should be limited to key words, ideas, and statistics. They should also contain speaking cues, little reminders about your delivery style. For instance, if you tend to fall into the trap of looking at your notes too frequently, you can put on the note card in bold letters: **STOP STARING AT ME**.

While we are on the topic of note cards, we encourage you to use note cards that fit neatly in your hand. Avoid using half or whole sheets of paper. We tell our students that there are few visual cues that audience members can see to signal the speaker's anxiety level. One of those cues is when the speaker's hands are shaking. Hand shaking is much more noticeable when you're holding a large sheet of paper in your hands.

Speak Loudly, Clearly, and With Conviction

So much of your message is carried by your voice. As Nancy Duarte puts it, "Your voice is multitalented." It can make you sound assertive, cautious, critical, humorous, motivational, sympathetic, or neutral. In business presentations, people often purposefully use a dispassionate, flat voice.[7] As we've said repeatedly throughout this book, emotions matter. A flat speaking voice does not make you sound objective; it makes you sound boring and dull. Use vocal variation by changing the pitch, rate, and tone of your voice to stress key points and create contrast. Practice your presentation and record those rehearsals when possible so that you can find and eliminate verbal fillers (e.g., "um") and find places to use your voice for impact. We discuss practice more thoroughly in the following text.

Move

Whenever possible, get away from the lectern (or podium). Remove barriers between you and your audience. Physical barriers may make you feel more comfortable, but they create distance between you and your audience. Remember that you are trying to have an engaging conversation. If you doubt our advice about the lectern, then try this simple test. The next time you go on a date, place a lectern on the table between you and your date. Let us know how the conversation goes. Instead of hiding behind a lectern, move (see Figure 6.3).

Movement has a number of excellent benefits. Not only does movement bring you closer to your audience, it also gives your body's nervous energy a healthy outlet. Nervous energy will find a way out. That's why people do strange things such as swaying side to side like a tree in the breeze or playing with their jewelry. Movement can also help you keep your presentation organized. For example, if your presentation has three

Figure 6.3 Speaker using movement to reduce barriers between him and the audience

main points, then you can identify each supporting point with an object in the room. Walk over to the first object, place your hand on it, and talk about the point associated with that object. When you are done making the first point, move to the second object and discuss the second object. And so on.

Dress Appropriately

We can't tell you exactly how to dress for a presentation. You have to know your audience. If all else fails, a conservative business suit often works. Just remember that your appearance sends a message to your audience. Match your appearance to the audience and situation.

Practice the Right Way

We want you to stop worrying so much about being perfect in your delivery style. Does that mean you should skip all the practice? No. We want you to be authentic, not lazy. Audiences will overlook minor flaws;

major flaws are another matter. You should practice. Practice will help you become more comfortable. You should, however, practice the right way. To learn the habits of good practice, we can learn from poor practice habits.

Some people never practice or never give themselves enough time to practice well. If you're the person who never practices, stop it. You're setting yourself up for failure. If you're the person who only practices once or twice the night before (or morning of) a presentation, stop it. You need time to practice. If you learn from your practice that you need to make major changes, you need time to make those changes and to practice more. Not practicing is not only inconsiderate, but it is not virtuous.

Some people do practice and even give themselves enough time to do so. Unfortunately, they either "rehearse" the presentation in their head without actually saying anything (not good for delivery) or fail to have an audience for their practice. If your goal as a speaker is to be authentic and to connect with your audience, then practicing in a room all by yourself is not terribly productive.

Some people practice in front of an audience, but they choose the wrong audience. These people gather friends, family members, or colleagues who are willing to listen to the rehearsal presentation but are not truly willing to give critical feedback. These rehearsal audience members simply tell you things like "It sounds great!" Although that's a nice boost to the ego, uncritical feedback does not help us to improve. In addition, when you have the wrong rehearsal audience, you take liberties that you wouldn't otherwise take. For example, when you make a minor error in front of the wrong rehearsal audience, you may stop and explain why you made the mistake and how you will fix it in the future or you may stop the presentation and start all over again. We strongly believe that once you start a rehearsal, you should move from start to finish without stopping.

Remember that no presentation is perfect. So why hold yourself to that standard? Forcing yourself to go from beginning to end without stopping replicates what the actual presentation will be like. You might as well get used to working through your mistakes. When you make a mistake, take a mental note and try to improve the next time through.

Designing and Using Multimedia Slides

Love it or hate it, multimedia slide design software, such as PowerPoint, Keynote, and Prezi, has become a part of the business presentation experience. As we mentioned earlier in this book, we have all been the victims of "death by PowerPoint," but we can't blame the software. We must blame those who use the software, including ourselves. Poor design is the result of poor planning, poor work habits, and (excuse our language) laziness.

The good news is that you have the power to fix what's wrong with your slide design. The better news is that you don't have to be a designer to make beautiful slides that have the appropriate impact on your audience. In this chapter, we give you some tips that you can put into practice immediately that will make your slides better. The ultimate takeaway from these tips is that less is more! For a more thorough treatment of slide design, we strongly recommend the following resources:

- *Presentation Zen: Simple Ideas on Presentation Design and Delivery* by Garr Reynolds
- *The Non-Designers Design Book* by Robin Williams

Overcoming Poor Planning, Poor Work Habits, and Laziness

We have been asked thousands of questions about slide design over the years. The most common questions include:

- How many bullet points are appropriate?
- How many words should I put on my slides?
- How many slides do I need to use?

The people who ask these questions are usually looking for concrete answers. Unfortunately, there are no simple answers. Slide design requires creative and critical thinking skills, and these skills require that you give yourself some time. *We usually tell people that they should start by asking whether they need multimedia slides at all.* Presenters often default to slides when they don't need them. Our answers to the questions in the preceding text usually end up looking something like this (in bullet point form):

- As many as you need to be clear, but not too many
- As many as you need to be clear, but not too many
- As many as you need to be clear, but not too many

How can it be that we live in a world where people hate bullet points and text-heavy slides and yet we are exposed to them almost daily? We do, in fact, have some simple answers to that question. First, people don't allow enough time for appropriate slide design. Too often, they try to design slides while also writing their presentation. These are two separate processes and should be treated as such. We urge you to write the presentation first and then design your slides. Second, people rely on PowerPoint default settings to guide them through the process. Consider Figure 6.4 that follows.

This is what you see when you open PowerPoint. Those bullet points are already there for you, like tantalizingly beautiful sirens calling out to you with their siren song. It's easy to simply fill in those bullets with words. Don't do it. It's a trap! Presentation shipwreck lies ahead.

How do you avoid falling into that trap? You should do what communication expert Garr Reynolds calls "planning analog." When planning your slides, use your imagination. Draw the slides. If they could look exactly as you want them, what would they look like? You don't have to be

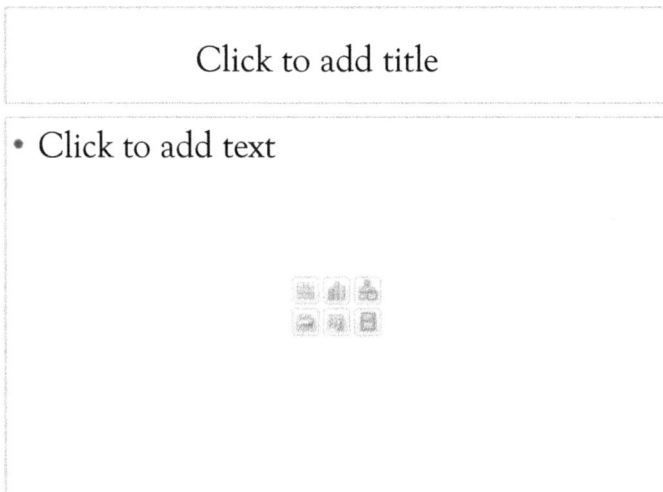

Figure 6.4 Default PowerPoint slide

an artist. Our drawings feature stick figures. To guide you in the process, you can print out a series of blank slides as a handout from PowerPoint. What you get are beautifully blank squares (see Figure 6.5) into which you can draw whatever content you like. Once you're satisfied with what you've drawn, open your slide design software and try to force it to create what you've drawn. This helps you avoid simply following the defaults.

Audiences also tend to dislike the overuse of SmartArt graphics, clip art, and background templates. They have become cliché, and they make you look like an unseasoned amateur. Instead, we encourage you to get creative and resourceful. Use high-quality pictures and images. You can take your own pictures or use one of the many resources online to find free or very low-cost stock photos.

It is important to remember that you are the presentation. The multimedia slides are there to evoke an emotional response from your audience and to support your message. The slides are not the message. Avoid overusing text and do not read from your slides! If you find that you must provide your audience with detailed information, lots of text, and tables crammed

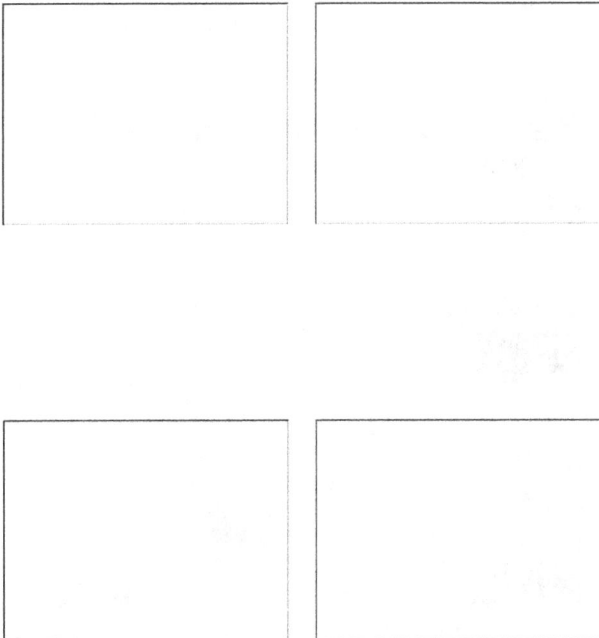

Figure 6.5 Blank PowerPoint slides for your planning

with data, then you need to produce a handout. Don't force the content onto your multimedia slides. Remember that your audience can only retain so much information and can pay attention to only so many stimuli. If they are busy reading your slides, they will not be listening to you.

The slide on the top side of Figure 6.6 was used in an actual presentation. It contains too many words. It uses a generic, clichéd background that has little to do with the topic of the presentation. It fails to make an emotional connection. Compare that to the slide on the bottom side of Figure 6.6. Do you see the difference?

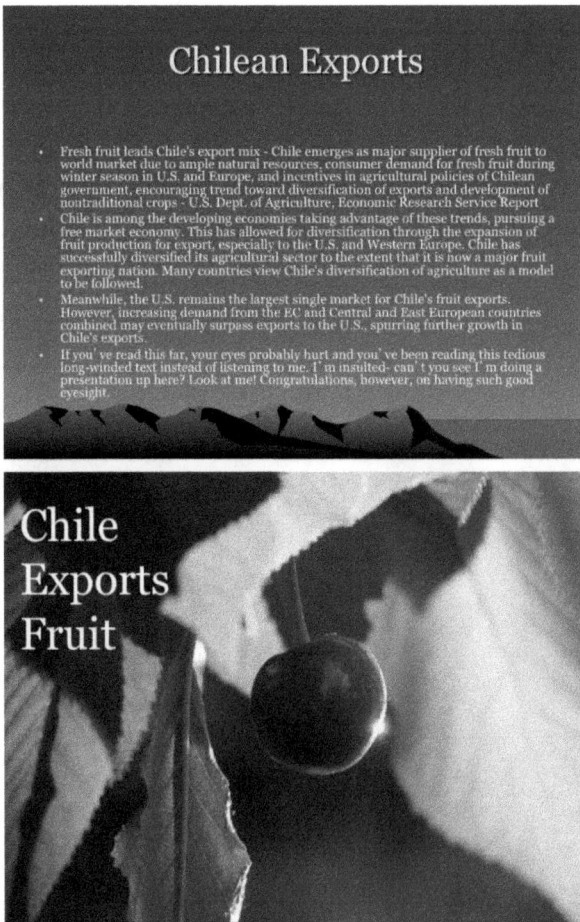

Figure 6.6 A slide that fails to evoke an emotional response and one that does[8]

Presenting with data can be tricky. We encourage—nay, demand—you to remember the less is more principle. When using data in your slides, carefully consider the point you are making with your data and present only enough data points to make that point. Any data that exceeds that threshold is just noise. It can actually distract from your point.

Consider the slide in Figure 6.7. Jason captured a picture of this slide during a presentation at our university. First, the slide displays so much data that it is nearly impossible to read. In fact, the speaker apologized for the small font. This happens frequently. Presenters produce poor slides and then apologize to the audience members.

Instead of making your audience members suffer through poorly produced slides, fix or eliminate them. When presenting with data, you have to consider font size. The data is useless if the audience can't see it.

You also need to consider what and how much data to present. The point of the slide in Figure 6.7 was that 54 students were within 30 credits of graduating and for some reason they left the university. Did all of that data really need to be presented in a slide? It is too much data and the font is too small. The data also doesn't do much to support the major point. In this case, the slide would look much better if it were converted to a handout. Jason snapped this picture because he realized that he was spending a great deal of time trying to read the slide and missed the point. He had to watch a video of the presentation to get the point.

Seniors who leave without graduating

Students status	2007 FTFT cohort		2008 FTFT cohort		2009 FTFT cohort	
	N	%	N	%	N	%
No longer enrolled with 90+ cumulative credits						
Administratively withdrawn	0	0	1	0	0	0
Did not notify us of intent to withdraw and did not register	61	4	64	5	50	4
Notified us of their intent to withdraw	10	1	12	1	4	0
Total no longer enrolled with 90+ cumulative credits	71	5	77	6	54	4
Graduated within 4 years	587	40	518	40	534	42
Graduated within 5 years	294	20	279	21	321	25
Graduated within 6 years	102	7	93	7	n/a	
Graduated within 7 years	35	2	n/a		n/a	
Enrolled fall 2015 (as of 8/18/15)	15	1	29	2	44	3
Total FTFT cohort	1469		1303		1281	

Figure 6.7 Multimedia slide with too much data

Another thing to consider when presenting with data is that you want your audience to be able to look at the data in a slide and very quickly draw the appropriate conclusion. The longer they think about the data, the less able they are to pay attention to what you have to say. Consider the slide in Figure 6.8 that follows.

Lisa snapped a picture of this slide about interest rates and the health of the economy. The presentation was interesting and intellectually engaging. The slides were, however, one notable exception. Look at the slide for five seconds. What's the point? Now imagine that you're trying to figure that out while a speaker is talking. Your odds of processing both the data and the content of the presentation are low. It's likely that this figure was copied from a written report without being reformatted for a presentation.

The slide on the top side of Figure 6.9 was another of Lisa's snapshots from the same presentation. The title of the slide does not make the point clear.

The vertical axis has too many major data points. The horizontal axis contains too many data points. This relatively good slide could be even better if left in the hands of a virtuous presenter. Compare the slide on the top side of Figure 6.9 with the one on the bottom side. Do you see how a few minor changes make the same data much clearer? Even though

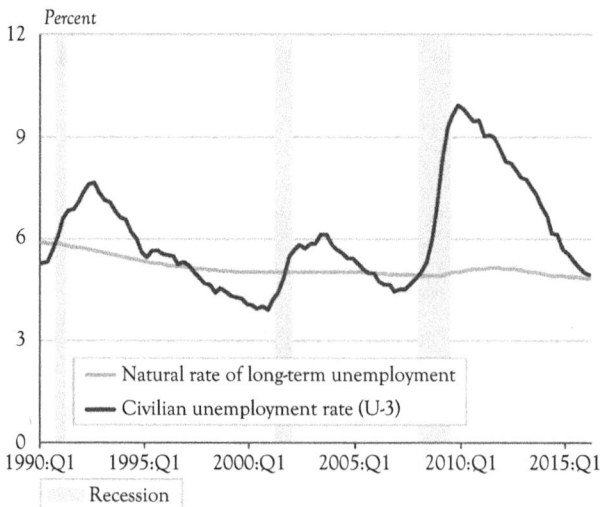

Figure 6.8 Sample slide where the point is not immediately clear[9]

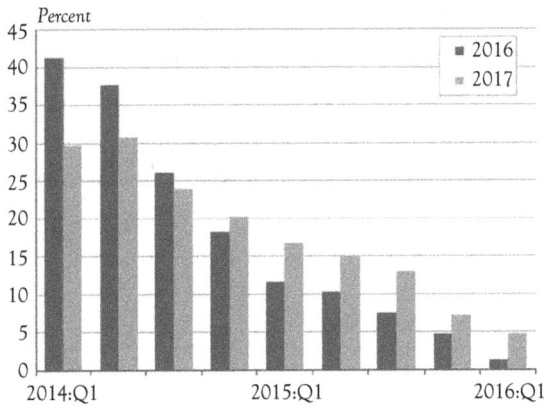

Forecasters increasingly believe unemployment
will stay below 6% in 2016 and 2017

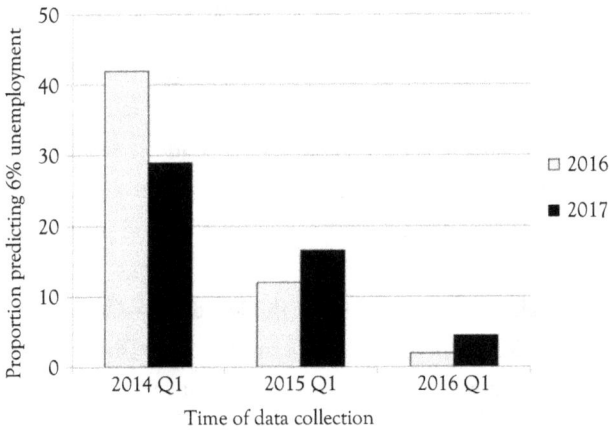

Figure 6.9 A "good" slide and a "virtuous" slide[10]

the slides contains fewer data points, you see a fairly clear linear trend in the data. In addition, the slide's title does a better job of conveying the slide's meaning.

Conclusion

In this, the book's final chapter, we provided you with a number of tips for becoming a "virtuous presenter." In particular, you should now know how to organize content for best results, develop an effective call to action, deliver with confidence, and build multimedia slides that won't bore your audience (see Box 6.4). Above all else, please remember that you are the presentation. As a finance professional, you are only asked to deliver a presentation because people in charge believe you know something that they do not. You are being given an opportunity. Don't squander that opportunity. Be bold and deliver a presentation that has real impact. Be a virtuous presenter.

Box 6.4 Chapter 6 takeaways

Be virtuous—Exhibit fortitude, prudence, justice, and temperance.

Capture the audience's attention—Even when you're an invited speaker, the audience may be distracted.

Organize for impact—Your audience can retain only so much information. So what do you want them to remember?

Call your audience to action—Make taking action easy for your audience.

Deliver with confidence—Be yourself. That advice is as good for presentations as it is for dating. Remember that you know what you're talking about. Your delivery will be enhanced if you practice the right way.

Design multimedia slides that get the job done—Go analog and try to make the slides look the way you want them to. The software should not tell you what to do. Tell the software what to do.

Notes

Chapter 1

1. V. Finelli, personal communication, January 24, 2016.
2. Hart Research Associates (2015).
3. National Association of Colleges and Employers (2015a).
4. National Association of Colleges and Employers (2015b).
5. Hart Research Associates (2015).
6. Elliott (2015).
7. Mcsween (2015).
8. Center for Professional Excellence (2014).
9. Center for Professional Excellence (2014).
10. Rikleen (2014).
11. Otey (2013).
12. Center for Professional Excellence (2015).
13. Anonymous, personal communication, February 18, 2016.
14. Center for Professional Excellence (2014).

Chapter 2

1. Grinols (2010).
2. Littlejohn and Foss (2011).
3. Buck and VanLear (2002).
4. Barnlund (1968).
5. Buck and VanLear (2002).
6. Berlo (1960).
7. Watt and VanLear (1996).
8. Rogers (1993).
9. Rogers (1993).
10. Middleton (2011).
11. Mankins, Brahm, and Caimi (2014).
12. Garber (2013).
13. Effectivemeetings.com (2013).
14. Harvard Business Review (2016).
15. Merrill (2012).
16. Harvard Business Review (2016).
17. C. Myles, personal communication, February 3, 2016.

18. Connie Myles (2016).
19. Mann (2006).
20. Warrell (2012).
21. Lindsay and Norman (1977).
22. Anonymous, personal communication, February 18, 2016.
23. Neiva and Hickson, III (2003).
24. Gallo (2016).
25. Snyder and Lee-Partridge (2013).
26. Purcell (2011).
27. McCarthy (2016).
28. Cline-Tomas and Chang (2016).
29. Hamilton and Hunter (1998).
30. Priester and Petty (2003).
31. Harrison (2015).
32. Sloat (2016).
33. Bolino, Varela, Bande, and Turnley (2006).
34. Hotten (2015).
35. Isidore (2015).

Chapter 3

1. R. Cassella, personal communication, February 18, 2016.
2. Heath and Heath (2007).
3. E. Bergenn, personal communication, February 21, 2016.
4. Snyder (2012).
5. Heath and Heath (2007).
6. Mayer and Salovey (1997).
7. Lam and Kirby (2002).
8. Lopes, Salovey, Cote, and Beers (2005).
9. Goleman (1995).
10. P. Bianco, personal communication, February 29, 2016.
11. Snyder and Lee-Partridge (2011).
12. Daft and Lengel (1984).
13. Gladwell (2008).
14. Harvard Business Review (2013).
15. Tannen (1995).

Chapter 4

1. This section is based on Snyder and Forbus (2014).
2. This section is based on Snyder and Forbus (2014).

3. Miller (1956).
4. This section based on Snyder and Forbus (2014).
5. Strunk and White (1979).
6. Gardner (2012).
7. Mills (2011).
8. Nordquist (2014).

Chapter 5

1. Hamilton and Mineo (1996).
2. This section is based on Cialdini (2007).

Chapter 6

1. Croston (2012).
2. J. Savini, personal communication, February 18, 2016.
3. This section is based on Duarte (2010) and Duarte (2012).
4. Reynolds (2012).
5. Brown (2012).
6. Brown (2010).
7. Duarte (2012).
8. Flickr photo courtesy of Ferreira (2007).
9. Rosengren (2016).
10. Rosengren (2016).

References

Barnlund, D. C. (1968). *Interpersonal communication: Survey and studies.* New York: Houghton Mifflin.

Berlo, D. (1960). *The process of communication: An introduction to theory and practice.* New York: Holt, Reinhart, and Winston.

Bolino, M. C., Varela, J. A., Bande, B., & Turnley, W. H. (2006). The impact of impression-management tactics on supervisor ratings of organizational citizenship behavior. *Journal of Organizational Behavior, 27*(3), 281–297. doi:10.1002/job.379

Brown, B. (2012). *Daring greatly: How the courage to be vulnerable transforms the way we live, love, parent, and lead.* New York: Avery.

Brown, B. (2010). The power of vulnerability. *TED Talks.* Retrieved from https://www.ted.com/talks/brene_brown_on_vulnerability?language=en

Buck, R., & VanLear, C. A. (2002). Verbal and nonverbal communication: Distinguishing symbolic, spontaneous, and pseudo-spontaneous nonverbal behavior. *Journal of Communication, 52*(3), 522–541. doi:10.1111/j.1460-2466.2002.tb02560.x

Center for Professional Excellence. (2014). *2014 National Professionalism Survey: Career Development Report.* Retrieved from http://www.ycp.edu/media/york-website/cpe/2014-National-Professionalism-Survey---Career-Development-Report.pdf

Center for Professional Excellence. (2015). *2015 National Professionalism Survey: Recent College Graduates Report.* Retrieved from http://www.ycp.edu/media/york-website/cpe/2015-National-Professionalism-Survey---Recent-College-Graduates-Report.pdf

Cialdini, R. B. (2007). *Influence: The psychology of persuasion* (revised ed.). New York: Harper Business.

Cline-Thomas, A., & Chang, D. (2016, February 17). Elementary school accidentally sends 'Hurt Feelings Report' to parents. *NBC Philadelphia.* Retrieved from http://www.nbcphiladelphia.com/news/local/Hurt-Feelings-Report-Lombardy-Elementary-School-Brandywine-School-District-Email-Delaware-369189861.html

Croston, G. (2012, November 29). The thing we fear more than death. *Psychology Today.* Retrieved from https://www.psychologytoday.com/blog/the-real-story-risk/201211/the-thing-we-fear-more-death

Daft, R. L., & Lengel, R. H. (1984). Information richness: A new approach to managerial behavior and organizational design. In L. L. Cummings, & B. M. Staw (Eds.), *Research in organizational behavior* (pp. 191–233). Homewood, IL: JAI Press.

Duarte, N. (2012). *Persuasive presentations: Inspire action, engage the audience, sell your ideas.* Cambridge, MA: Harvard Business Review Press.

Duarte, N. (2010). *Resonate: Present visual stories that transform audiences.* Hoboken, NJ: Wiley.

Elliott, M. (2015, May 3). 5 skills college grads need to get a job. *USA Today.* Retrieved from http://www.usatoday.com/story/money/personal finance/2015/05/03/cheat-sheet-skills-college-grads-job/26574631/

Estimate the cost of a meeting with this calculator. (2016, January 11). *Harvard Business Review.* Retrieved from https://hbr.org/2016/01/estimate-the-cost-of-a-meeting-with-this-calculator

Ferreira, A. (2007, December 12). Flickr photo. Retrieved from http://www.flickr.com/photos/annais/2136522231/

Gallo, C. (2016, March 31). 40 years later, Steve Jobs' success secrets still apply to aspiring leaders. *Forbes.* Retrieved from http://www.forbes.com/sites/carminegallo/2016/03/31/40-years-later-steve-jobs-success-secrets-still-apply-to-aspiring-leaders/#3ab97e029b75

Garber, M. (2013, February 10). You probably write a novel's worth of e-mail every year. *The Atlantic.* Retrieved from http://www.theatlantic.com/technology/archive/2013/01/you-probably-write-a-novels-worth-of-email-every-year/266942/

Gardner, B. A. (2012). *HBR guide to better business writing.* Cambridge: Harvard Business Press.

Gladwell, M. (2008). *Outliers: The story of success.* Boston, MA: Little, Brown, and Company.

Goleman, D. (1995). *Emotional intelligence: Why it can matter more than IQ.* New York: Bantam.

Grinols, A. (2010). *The last lecture: 7 values of effective communicators.* Presented at the 2010 Convention of the Association for Business Communication, Chicago, IL.

Hamilton, M. A., & Hunter, J. E. (1998). The effect of language intensity on receiver evaluations of message, source, and topic. In M. Allen, & R. W. Preiss (Eds.), *Persuasion: Advances through meta-analysis* (pp. 99–138). Cresskill, NJ: Hampton Press.

Hamilton, M. A., & Mineo, P. J. (1996). Personality and persuasibility: Developing a multidimensional model of belief systems. *World Communication, 24,* 1–16.

Harrison, V. (2015, August 3). Libor scandal trader Tom Hayes jailed for 14 years. *CNN Money.* Retrieved from http://money.cnn.com/2015/08/03/news/libor-scandal-tom-hayes-jail/

Hart Research Associates. (2015). *Falling short? College learning and career success*. Retrieved from https://www.aacu.org/sites/default/files/files/LEAP/2015employerstudentsurvey.pdf

Heath, C., & Heath, D. (2007). *Made to stick: Why some ideas survive and others die*. New York: Random House.

Hotten, R. (2015, December 10). Volkswagen: The scandal explained. *BBC News*. Retrieved from http://www.bbc.com/news/business-34324772

Isidore, C. (2015, December 10). VW chief: Scandal is 'hard to believe'. *CNN Money*. Retrieved from http://www.bbc.com/news/business-34324772

Lam, L. T., & Kirby, S. L. (2002). Is emotional intelligence an advantage? An exploration of the impact of emotional and general intelligence on individual performance. *The Journal of Social Psychology, 142*(1), 133–143.

Lindsay, P., & Norman, D. A. (1977). *Human information processing: An introduction to psychology* (2nd ed.). New York: Academic Press.

Littlejohn, S. W., & Foss, K. A. (2011). *Theories of human communication* (10th ed.). Belmont, CA: Wadsworth.

Lopes, P. N., Salovey, P., Cote, S., & Beers, M. (2005). Emotion regulation abilities and the quality of social interaction. *Emotion, 5*(1), 113–118.

Mankins, M. C., Brahm, C., & Caimi, G. (2014, May). Your scarcest resource. *Harvard Business Review*. Retrieved from https://hbr.org/2014/05/your-scarcest-resource

Mann, M. (2006, February 21). Running more productive meetings. *43 Folders*. Retrieved from http://www.43folders.com/2006/02/21/meetings

Mayer, J. D., & Salovey, P. (1997). What is emotional intelligence? In P. Salovey, & D. Sluyter (Eds.), *Emotional development and emotional intelligence: Educational implications* (pp. 3–31). New York: Basic Books.

McCarthy, A. (2016, February 6). Hillary's e-mail recklessness compromised our national security. *National Review*. Retrieved from http://www.nationalreview.com/article/430879/hillary-clinton-email-scandal-assume-intelligence-compromised?target=topic&tid=4571

McSween, D. (2015). Finance job skills. *Houston Chronicle Online*. Retrieved from http://work.chron.com/finance-job-skills-12948.html

Merrill, D. (2012, August 17). Why multitasking doesn't work. *Forbes*. Retrieved from http://www.forbes.com/sites/douglasmerrill/2012/08/17/why-multitasking-doesnt-work/

Middleton, D. (2011, March 3). Students struggle for words: Business schools put more emphasis on writing amid employer complaints. *Wall Street Journal Online*. Retrieved from http://online.wsj.com/article/SB10001424052748703409904576174651780110970.html

Miller, G. A. (1956). The magical number seven, plus or minus two: Some limits on our capacity for processing information. *Psychological Review, 63*(2), 81–97. doi:10.1037/h0043158

Mills, B. (2011, August 5). Compound subjects. *Grammar Girl.* Retrieved from http://www.quickanddirtytips.com/education/grammar/compound-subjects

National Association of Colleges and Employers. (2015a). *Job outlook 2016: Attributes employers want to see on new college graduates' resumes.* Retrieved from http://www.naceweb.org/s11182015/employers-look-for-in-new-hires. aspx

National Association of Colleges and Employers. (2015b). *Career readiness defined.* Retrieved from http://www.naceweb.org/knowledge/career-readiness-competencies.aspx

Neiva, E., & Hickson III, M. (2003). Deception and honesty in animal and human communication: A new look at communicative interaction. *Journal of Intercultural Research, 32*(1), 23–45.

Nordquist, R. (2014). 200 common redundancies. *About.com.* Retrieved from http://grammar.about.com/od/words/a/redundancies.htm

Otey, B. S. (2013). Millennials, technology, and professional responsibility: Training a new generation in technological professionalism. *Journal of the Legal Profession,* 37, 201–264.

Priester, J. R., & Petty, R. E. (2003). The influence of spokesperson trustworthiness on message elaboration, attitude strength, and advertising effectiveness. *Journal of Consumer Psychology, 13*(4), 408–421. doi: 10.1207/S15327663JCP1304_08

Purcell, K. (2011). Search and email still top the list of most popular online activities. *Pew Internet and American Life Project.* Retrieved from http://www.pewinternet.org/Reports/2011/Search-and-email/Report.aspx

Reynolds, G. (2012). *Presentation zen: Simple ideas on presentation design and delivery.* Berkeley, CA: New Riders.

Rikleen, L. S. (2014, February). Millennials and technology in today's workplace. *PD Quarterly.* Retrieved from http://rikleeninstitute.com/sites/default/files/images/rikleen.14millennials.pdf

Rogers, E. (1993). *A history of communication study: A biographical approach.* New York: Free Press.

Rosengren, E. S. (2016). *Are financial markets too pessimistic about the economy?* Presentation delivered at Central Connecticut State University. Retrieved from https://www.bostonfed.org/news/speeches/rosengren/2016/041816/041816figuresandcomments.pdf

Sloat, S. (2016, April 22). Volkswagen posts deep loss after taking $18.28 billion hit on emissions scandal. *Morningstar.* Retrieved from https://www.morningstar.com/news/dow-jones/TDJNDN_201604227225/volkswagen-posts-deep-loss-after-taking-1828-billion-hit-on-emissions-scandal.html

Snyder, J. L. (2012). Extending the empathic communication model of burnout: Incorporating individual differences to learn more about workplace emotion, communicative responsiveness, and burnout. *Communication Quarterly, 60*(1), 122–142.

Snyder, J. L., & Forbus, R. (2014). *Today's business communication: A how-to guide for the modern professional.* New York: Business Expert Press.

Snyder, J. L., & Lee-Partridge, J. (2013). Understanding communication channel choice in team knowledge sharing. Manuscript accepted for publication in *Corporate Communications: An International Journal, 18*(4), 417–431.

Snyder, J. L., & Lee-Partridge, J. (2011). Employee media choices when sharing knowledge in work teams: A test of the layered model. Manuscript published in the *Proceedings of the Association for Business Communication.* Available at: http://businesscommunication.org/conventions/abc-convention-proceedings/2011-annual-convention-proceedings/

Strunk, W., & White, E. B. (1979). *The elements of style* (3rd ed.). London: Macmillan.

Tannen, D. (1995). The power of talk: Who gets heard and why. *Harvard Business Review, 73*(5), 138–148.

The state of meetings today. (2013). *EffectiveMeetings.com.* Retrieved from http://www.effectivemeetings.com/meetingbasics/meetstate.asp

Warrell, M. (2012, August). Hiding behind email? Four times you should never use email. *Forbes.* Retrieved from http://www.forbes.com/sites/margiewarrell/2012/08/27/do-you-hide-behind-email/

Watt, J. H., & VanLear, C. A. (1996). *Dynamic patterns in communication processes.* Thousand Oaks, CA: Sage.

Women in the workplace: A research roundup. (2013, September). *Harvard Business Review.* Retrieved from https://hbr.org/2013/09/women-in-the-workplace-a-research-roundup

Index

OTHER TITLES IN OUR CORPORATE COMMUNICATION COLLECTION

Debbie DuFrene, Stephen F. Austin State University, Editor

- *Technical Marketing Communication: A Guide to Writing, Design, and Delivery* by Emil B. Towner and Heidi L. Everett
- *Managerial Communication for the Arabian Gulf* by Valerie Priscilla Goby, Catherine Nickerson, and Chrysi Rapanta
- *The Language of Success: The Confidence and Ability to Say What You Mean and Mean What You Say in Business and Life* by Kim Wilkerson and Alan Weiss
- *Writing for Public Relations: A Practical Guide for Professionals* by Janet Mizrahi
- *Managing Virtual Teams, Second Edition* by Debbie D. DuFrene and Carol M. Lehman
- *Planning and Organizing Business Reports: Written, Oral, and Research-Based* by Dorinda Clippinger
- *Writing for the Workplace: Business Communication for Professionals* by Janet Mizrahi
- *Get Along, Get It Done, Get Ahead: Interpersonal Communication in the Diverse Workplace* by Geraldine E. Hynes
- *Writing Online: A Guide to Effective Digital Communication at Work* by Erika Darics

Announcing the Business Expert Press Digital Library

Concise e-books business students need for classroom and research

This book can also be purchased in an e-book collection by your library as

- a one-time purchase,
- that is owned forever,
- allows for simultaneous readers,
- has no restrictions on printing, and
- can be downloaded as PDFs from within the library community.

Our digital library collections are a great solution to beat the rising cost of textbooks. E-books can be loaded into their course management systems or onto students' e-book readers.
The **Business Expert Press** digital libraries are very affordable, with no obligation to buy in future years. For more information, please visit **www.businessexpertpress.com/librarians**. To set up a trial in the United States, please email **sales@businessexpertpress.com**.

www.ingramcontent.com/pod-product-compliance
Lightning Source LLC
Chambersburg PA
CBHW071905200326
41519CB00016B/4511